Praise for Mzee Ali

"His tale of slaving and soldiering, told in the first person, is graphic, action-filled and revealing"
James Mitchell, *Star*

"Mzee Ali's story, while personal, also reveals glimpses of Tanzania's history. His biography is full of adventure and a point of view that is quite different to a Western and European outlook that makes for fascinating reading"
Ingrid Smit, The Write Co.

"... this is a fascinating insight into what it was like living in Africa in the late 1800s and early twentieth century"
Daily News

"This is a powerfully evocative account of Mzee Ali's life ... This book truly offers a closer, personal look at the people who helped build a kaleidoscope of history in Africa. It is a worthwhile read"
Get It! Durban West

Dear Les & Richard

Thank you for a wonderful stay and for spoiling me.

MZEE *Ali*

The biography of an African slave-raider turned *askari* & scout

Bror Ürme MacDonell
with Kerrin Cocks

13/04

30° South Publishers

Other books by Kerrin Cocks
I won't be home next summer (co-author)
Africa@War Vol. XX Rhodesian Fire Force, 1966–1980

First published in 2006

This edition published in 2015 by:
30° SOUTH PUBLISHERS (PTY) LTD.
16 Ivy Road, Pinetown 3610
South Africa
www.30degreessouth.co.za
info@30degreessouth.co.za

ISBN 978-1-928211-63-1

Design and origination by SA Publishing Services
Cover design by SA Publishing Services / kerrincocks@gmail.com
Printed and bound by Pinetown Printers (Pty) Ltd.

From lightning and tempest;
from plague, pestilence, and
famine; from locusts, murrain,
and drought; from battle
and murder, and from dying
suddenly and unprepared,
"Good Lord, deliver us."
— *The Litany*

NOTE FROM THE PUBLISHER

Mzee Ali has been a labour of love. Gavin MacDonell first approached me with his late father's manuscript in early 2005 and gave me the background to this remarkable account of a grand old man of Africa. In the late 1940s, Bror Ürme MacDonell was employed in the British colonial service by the Department of Locust Control, covering southern Tanganyika and the northeastern corner of Northern Rhodesia. It was here in the bush, around the campfire at night and listening to the stories of his lead scout, that he had the presence of mind to take notes.

The notebooks emerged some fifteen years later in 1963 while Bror was living in Salisbury, Southern Rhodesia. He began writing Mzee Ali in longhand and, a decade later, dictated the account to Stella Townsend, who faithfully typed the manuscript, with her comments that the text was too factual and lacked colour. She was right, but at the time Bror's primary aim was to get the facts down. Here, the publishers, on behalf of the author's family, would like to express their heartfelt thanks and gratitude to Stella.

When Gavin gave me Stella's typed-up manuscript I read it in one sitting, through the night till dawn. It absorbed me totally and I knew we had something that was wonderfully unique. I passed the manuscript on to my wife and partner, Kerrin, and she too read it in a single sitting, with her comments (like Stella's) that the manuscript needed a significant rewrite in order to bring the story alive. And that's what she did, solidly for three months—she transcribed the text electronically and at the same time rewrote the story of Mzee Ali, making it her own and drawing on her personal experiences of Tanzania and its wonderful people. She faced some daunting challenges, not least of which was trying to untangle the confusing timelines of Mzee Ali's youth in the closing decades of the 19th century. (The Western calendar differs from the Islamic calendar, neither of which a century ago held meaning to an African's interpretation of time and past.) Place names and spellings have also changed in a century and tracing the routes of the slavers and of the German *askaris* of World War I was no easy task. However, Kerrin's greatest challenge was to get inside the mind of Mzee Ali, and I believe she has produced something very special.

Inevitably, the story has been drawn with an element of licence. However, the facts, as related by Mzee to the author, have been faithfully reproduced. But memory dims with time and some as have been recorded may be historically inaccurate. This is unimportant—what matters is that a miniscule speck of Africa's vast, untapped history, the story of one man has been written down. On a continent where the past and its traditions are passed down through song and story-telling, Mzee Ali stands out as a written tribute to a long-forgotten era that captures the richness, the beauty, the cruelty ... and the very soul of Africa.

Our hope is that Mzee Ali will transport you back to a time and place of long ago—on a safari or by a campfire—and that you will come away with the same feelings of warmth and respect that we have experienced.

Chris Cocks
Johannesburg, February 2006

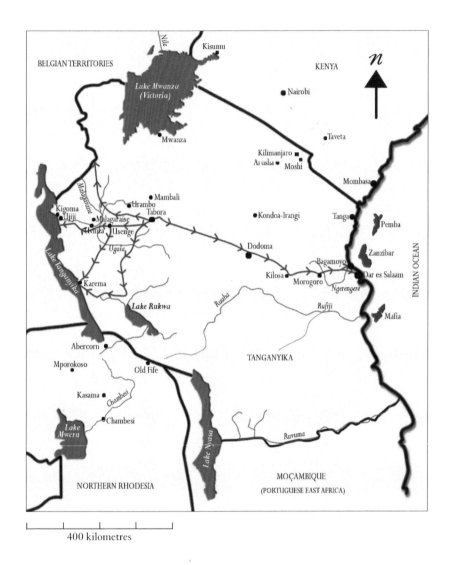

400 kilometres

Slave-trade route, circa 1890

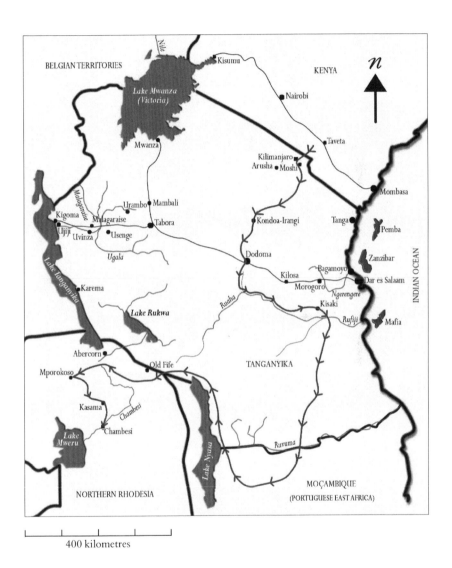

Askari route, 1915–1918

PROLOGUE

I wrote the story of Mzee Ali from notes while on safari in some of the most remote and infrequently visited parts of western Tanganyika (now Tanzania), sitting around the campfire in the company of locust scouts, of whom Mzee was a member.

Much of the country, because of the rough terrain and absence of roads, was traversed on foot with porters to carry the expedition's requirements. Mzee's presence on these ventures into this unknown, unmapped and unsurveyed country was essential. Mzee had many years' experience in this type of work and an unrivalled knowledge of the bush; at times it seemed he could literally smell a distant water point.

On a more personal level it was Mzee who encouraged me to explore further into these wilds and delve deeper into the memories of an old grey-haired gentleman's mind, the mind of a noble African generation.

Mzee told his story as the truth and there was little or no reason to disbelieve its authenticity. He stood tall and strong, his years etched on his face and his life etched on his soul—the figure of courage, strength and loyalty. He remained calm and clear-minded when our camp was visited at night by unwelcome lions, or by an elephant breaking the bough of the tree under which we slept. He had been raised not to panic when the unexpected happened. In his early years he was taught and expected to bring order to a confused and frightened army of porters, slaves and scouts, awoken in the same manner.

My final farewell to this fine old man of wild Africa was while camping in the bush some twenty miles from Usenge. I raised my glass and toasted the 'Old People' of Africa—the people who had helped build a kaleidoscope of history in Africa … and to Mzee Ali Kalikilima.

Standing, as always, erect with great dignity on a bright moonlit night, he turned, shook hands and said, "Kwa heri bwana." He took a moment to survey the campsite and the many people sitting around the blazing fire, as if trying to read the future in the tongues of the flames or shadows cast against a nearby anthill, and said goodbye to his companions.

The rolling sound of a lion's roar coming from a long way off, the bark of a scrounging jackal nearby, the laugh of hyena and the distant trumpet of an elephant, seemed to draw the curtain closed behind the fading figure of a true man, returning to his home to rest.

He is, and was, Africa. May Allah grant him sanctuary in his heaven.

Bror Ürme MacDonell

PART I

1

The penetrating and, at times, unbearable African sun had long since been forced into oblivion; dusk folded into night with only the stars providing sufficient light by which to see. The birds of the day had gone to sleep or roost and the night was coming alive—as only it can in the raw heart of the bush. The roar of the insects, the birds that survived by prowling the night and the larger, more commonly thought-of animals, had woken from their slumber to serenade the darkness—each tone, each pitch, so clearly understood by one another—a mating call, a warning or the barely inaudible snap of a twig.

And so, almost simultaneously, had the night's camp life been roused. There were no tents to be erected, just a camping bed beneath the invaluable mosquito net, a camp chair and table set and, not too far away, a big campfire, around which moved the shadows of the African staff. These were the members of the safari, eight or ten of them—scouts, lorry drivers, cooks—all moving this way and that, preparing the evening meal. Others were cutting up and laying in stock quantities of necessary firewood for the night or making ready their places to sleep.

My meal, always cooked separately in its own special place, was not quite ready. There was the usual babble around the fire, squabbles about who was going to cook, who was going to sleep where. Arrangements were made for who was going to wake up at what time in the night to stoke the fire, always forgetting that such arrangements were never really necessary as this was automatically done by whoever happened to wake and feel chilled by the cold night air.

Sundown in the African bush is an eerily enchanting time—the endless ring of the cicada beetles has died down and the night's symphony has not yet begun. The periods just after sunset and just before sunrise are strangely silent. Sitting by the fire you relax completely and a gentle serenity engulfs you, luring your mind toward dreams—dreams of the happenings in the bush, dreams of people and places and of the past—Africa's past, its tribes, its secrets. I found contentment at sundown, surrounded by the familiar faces, black as can be found, who had seen trials and passed through tribulations. But of this wealth of life, few had experienced so much as 'the old-timer' … the Mzee.

So it was, while sitting on a petrol box, staring into the fire and sipping a well-deserved drink, that old Mzee, his exact age unknown, but I put him somewhere in his seventies, began to share his history. The past gradually unfurled into a thousand images thrown as shadows by the tongues of flickering flames, devouring a piece of wood some hundred years old.

Staring into the campfire, as though the flames were turning themselves into the pictures of his past, he sat on his haunches, his wrinkled chin resting on the back of his sinewy old hands, folded over his knees. Although completely grey, his face lined with age, Mzee's eyes were alert, clear and observant, always quietly watching. Despite his years his body had a youthfulness about it, an endurance sprung from a great inner strength. It seemed he had forgotten there were others around him as he began re-living his past in all the detail he could remember and describe. Slowly, with one memory pushing forward another he told of his childhood in the country of Unyamwezi—the People of the Moon. He was of the Wanyanyembe tribe.

As he spoke the flames licked higher, twisting themselves into old Mzee's story. His voice seemed to take on the timbre of his youth and so he spoke …

"The country was so wild in those days, it's hard to imagine now just how wild it was."

His gaze grew distant as he spoke, slipping deeper into his past.

᠅᠅᠅

There were houses dotted here and there, not the types one sees today, but those which we all helped build from the things that God gave us—trees, bark and string from the bark of other trees. Poles were securely tied together, making up the skeleton of the round pole-and-mud house, grass was used for thatching and mud filled the walls.

My father started building in the village of Kaze, near what is today known as Tabora. It took about a week of us all building, starting at first light and working until the blessed darkness gave us a welcome reprieve, only to begin again at daybreak. When the time came for plastering it goes without saying that as children we took more interest than usual. The mud was made from a certain kind of anthill, which was hoed down and mixed with water to make *potopot*, a kind of mud-clay from which we not only made mud for plastering, but also moulded into effigies of cattle, people, or anything else that came to our imagination or for the games that were in vogue at the time.

The act of building such a house, the labour, staying with friends while building was underway and the excitement of finally moving in, is symbolic of setting down roots. Permanent roots, unshakable by the advancement of time or the brutality of man—roots to which one will always return.

When the house was finished we could return to the important business of being children—the village was our playground and our playground had many forms. At times some of us were lions, fierce and cocky—others were the cattle, herded by a watchful boy. The lions would try to steal and kill the cattle, while the herd boy had to raise the alarm and brave the lions, chasing them away. We would also have to tend and graze our parents' cattle—this job was shared between my brothers and me under the watchful supervision of my father.

As a youth my father had embraced Islam and was thus in great favour with the Arab settlers. He was a wealthy nobleman.

Time went on and when I was of age, about fourteen years old, my father instructed me in the art of shooting with a muzzle-loader gun, the only modern, manufactured type of weapon we could get. The guns were brought in by the Arabs as trading goods for slaves and ivory—not to mention the wealth of colourful cloths and materials, beads, mirrors, wire bangles, pots and many other things they used for trading.

This was a proud time for me, to be taken under my father's wing … a metamorphosis. No longer was I the boy hiding in the low shrubs, planning an attack on an 'unsuspecting cow'. I felt a head and shoulders taller than that boy. I was becoming a man, partaking in the business of men.

A few months later I was instructed by my father to embark upon my first safari, on my own. For this I was supplied with twenty guns, eighteen kegs of gunpowder, thirty boxes of percussion caps for the guns, bales of cloth, rolls of wire and boxes of beads—all for the purpose of bartering and buying slaves. A hefty charge for a young man. My father's wealth and status had bought him some hundred slaves, mostly young men and women, and of course the inevitable number of concubines, all denoting his high estate.

I had previously accompanied my father on a few safaris before undertaking this coming-of-age journey. So I was familiar with the routine of such a safari. I had learned to barter with the chiefs of the villages from whom slaves and ivory could be bought. I understood the haggling that had to take place and knew how to check physique, teeth, looks, age and whether puberty had been reached by both male and female, or not. I knew how to look after the slaves on the road and keep them under control. I knew how to organize their feeding. This was one of the big problems as food had to be carried for them and the guards, as well as the many other items required on safaris of such a nature.

So it was, that early one morning—the first light pink in the dust in front of my hut—my chief captain of the slave labour force called on me to start on this baptismal journey—a safari to buy slaves and ivory deep in the Tanganyikan bush. We were to march in a southwesterly direction to the village of Mtakuja, close to the shores of Lake Tanganyika, where it was known—from reports from other traders—that considerable numbers of slaves could be bought and that ivory was to be found in large quantities.

I rose, little caring about the noise I made, leaving the hut with more confidence than I felt. Showing any fear would have jeopardized the safari but soon the excitement and traditional farewell greetings to my family quelled the nervousness that rippled inside me.

Outside, everything was meticulously laid out, ready, with each slave and labourer standing by his load, which I carefully checked as my father had taught me. When I was satisfied that all was well I gave the order to load up and get into marching order—taking command of this, my first trading safari. Certain trusted slaves and soldiers of my guard, all armed with muzzle-loaders, distributed themselves down the column of porters to ensure that nobody tried to run away or discard his load, or at least a part of it in order to lighten his burden.

At times I was carried on a *mashila*, a type of stretcher tied between two poles, borne by four slaves who were relieved at intervals. At other times I walked in front of the long line of porters, depending on whether we were nearing a village or not. It was not dignified to walk when one was the owner of such great wealth and so many slaves. The going was relatively slow, the porters had to be encouraged with whips to maintain a steady pace. The path was well worn and at that stage it was not necessary to hack back the bush to clear one, as it would later be. As the day wore on the heat intensified, as did the pitch of the cicada beetles, shrill and incessant—a constant reminder that here we were at Africa's mercy. Control over our lives and the success of my safari had been torn from my hands and placed firmly in hers, and in those of the volatile tribes we were yet to encounter. Out here one had to be constantly aware, in tune to every sound, every movement—even a change in the wind direction could be crucial. My father's training had been thorough and I relied solely on this and my keen sense of observation.

The first village we came to was about six hours' walk from Tabora, a recognized stop for any safari southbound from Tabora. It was the village of Rashidi bin (son of) Ngomani. He was known to all and likewise, knew all. By some unknown means he always knew when a safari was nearing his village. He knew also what the safari comprised and who the leader was, thus enabling him to assess the bounty he could demand as a safeguard for travelling through his country. The usual negotiations that took place at such a meeting were preceded by a salute of guns, fired to inform the village that a safari was approaching. This was done when the safari was still some miles away. The villagers would line our route for about half a mile, singing traditional songs of welcome, murmuring respectful greetings as I passed. The chief would have delegated a representative to welcome the strangers and escort us into his village.

Jambo. Habari ya safari? (Good day, how is your journey?) was the standard greeting. When the formalities were taken care of the villagers would cheerfully assist in carrying the heavy loads, knowing that a fair amount of what we had brought with us would stay behind. People would keenly enquire as to the news from

Tabora. Discussions of a simple nature would ensue, such as how were the local flocks of sheep and goats; who had married whom, thus slowly bringing the question of the safari and its possessions into the discussion and the estimated value of the goods being carried. It was important to ascertain how much accommodation was required for the night and how many additional meals would need to be prepared. A levy was then estimated and a request put forward for its equivalent to be paid in goods, thus allowing the safari to stay the night, to be well fed and protected. It goes without saying that these negotiations always led to some form of bartering which could take hours, but a price was always eventually agreed upon—one side having come down in its price and the other side having gone up.

The chief was an amenable man; he knew the value of his hospitality but also the danger in taking advantage of a safari led by the son of a highly respected nobleman. He made sure that our night was comfortable and that my guards and I were well taken care of by the women in the village, their services being included in the negotiated price. The slaves were fed and rounded up. They spent the night guarded by sentries posted at intervals around the camp in case of desertion, or attack.

Though it was strictly not according to the teachings of Islam, inevitably a couple of pots of beer were produced after the campfires were lit and the food was put on to cook. The beer quenched our thirst and worked marvellously as a sedative for a good night's rest.

The next morning, after an early rise and payment for the night's accommodation with three kegs of gunpowder, a couple of bales of cloth, a roll of wire, a few mirrors, a handful of beads and other items, the safari was allowed to proceed on its way. A salute of guns and the festive singing and dancing of the women and young girls of the village accompanied our departure. Again they lined our route, their bare feet gently thumping out the rhythm of their tune in the red earth, the dust rising around them as they sang, dissolving in the early dawn.

The *wapagazii* (porters) were escorted by the usual armed, loyal slaves and paid servants. They were of many different tribes, captured from numerous raids and buying safaris that my father had made on the WaUfipa, the WaRungwa, WaMpingdwi and WaUha. And so the second day started, the crisp harmonies and pulsating dance strains of the women still lingering in the air around us.

The dew was heavy on the long, unburned grass—it was cold and uncomfortable, soaking our clothes as we brushed it aside from the footpath that was slowly becoming more and more overgrown the farther we travelled from the village. The sun was up, but at such an early hour it has little effect on the dew.

The sun was the clock for game and humans alike—all our estimations of time were based on its position. To us, the twenty-four-hour day as you know it, was in fact two days—the day of sun or light and the day of night—which was naturally very difficult to measure unless the moon was full. On any other night it was measured by the crow of the first rooster, *njogoro ya kwanza*, which could be at any time from three in the morning to dawn. *Njogoro ya pili* was the second rooster crow of the night, or true dawn.

This second crow marked our time for waking on the third

morning. The day's walk was to be a long one—about twenty-five miles—through very wild country, the type of country one could not predict, could not anticipate. The type of country that would tear your safari apart if you let your guard down for just the briefest of moments.

11

The seasonal grass fires had mostly charred the thick woodland. Only small patches remained unscathed. The going was slow, the clumps of burnt grass were painful and awkward to walk on and the porters complained bitterly. As we painstakingly picked our way over this scorched earth, the reality of fire stretched only as far as our carefully placed bare feet. In truth, fire was to be our biggest enemy, for we safaried in the hot, dry months before the coming of the late summer rains.

At around midday we were walking along the recognized track to the village of Ysusfu. This is the time of day when the heat is at its most exhaustive and the placing of one foot in front of the other is more out of habit and momentum than conscious thought. We moved as if in sleep, the unrelenting heat robbing us of our keen senses, letting down our guard. Obviously this blanket heat affected the *wapagazii* more than it did the rest of us, because of the heavy loads they carried, loads that became heavier with every step. Thus it made sense to travel in the morning and afternoon, and rest at midday. The porters were allowed to unburden themselves in an orderly fashion. Some were instructed to cook; others were escorted into the bush to relieve themselves while others were allowed, still under escort, to wander in the nearby bush to look for wild fruit. Sentries were strategically placed along the track, although desertion was becoming less of an option for the slaves as the density and wildness of the bush intensified.

Desertion was not the only danger though—there was no telling what might happen—our heavily laden safari would be a very tempting target to an opportunistic local. It could easily have been spotted by local tribesmen who might think it more than worth their while to chance their luck and launch an attack—the wealth, should they be victorious, would be great.

It was during this state of half-wake–half-sleep that the first alarm was raised of a raging fire tearing through the dry bush towards us, in the direction from which we'd just come.

When my father had instructed me in the technique of safaris, he had taught me how to keep control of the slave labour force, when and where to place sentries while walking and when resting. I had observed him closely on previous safaris when he had bartered with the tribal chiefs for accommodation, slaves and ivory. My tutelage in musketry had been thorough and extensive. However, when journeying deep into the bush there are a host of other incidents and dangers for which one must be prepared.

As a young boy, I had witnessed my father in action, as time after time the bush threw various dangerous challenges at the safari. He never panicked, never showed the slightest hint of fear. He always handled the situation deftly, taking as much care to safeguard the members of the safari as he did the valuable cargo they carried. It was drummed into me that more dangerous than an angry elephant bull or a hostile tribe, was fear. Fear drove you to panic and once panic had set in you would lose control and never regain it. Don't lose your head. Be practical and methodical.

My father's voice now flooded my mind as I grappled to stay calm. His steady, authoritative voice issuing orders doused my fears and cleared my head. The first thing that had to be done was to clear the long grass around the safari as quickly as possible, to prevent the fire reaching the goods—and us. Orders were issued and we set about hacking at the grass with *pangas*. This was a task to which the whole gang was put, irrespective of position, except for myself, as I controlled operations and had to be protected at all costs.

Regardless of our efforts, the heat was intensifying, the fire moving much faster than we had initially thought, catching up with the grass-cutting. The process of cutting back took time and labour as the cuttings had to be stacked well away from the proximity of the goods. The heat was now becoming unbearable. Although temporarily out of danger our eyes watered from the thickening smoke, making work virtually impossible. Not another moment could be wasted and the order was given to collect as many of the goods as possible—especially the gunpowder and weaponry—and place them all into the cleared area. Some men were left to carry on cutting and moving the cut grass away from the clearing. The fire was out of control. It moved toward us with a fury I had never experienced and suddenly our island within its flames seemed hopelessly inadequate. Drenched with perspiration, blinded by the smoke, the safari teetered on the verge of hysteria. To keep a firm hand on the men I continued issuing instructions, hoping these simple actions would keep their minds focused—away from the impending danger. Unable to withstand the searing heat members of the gang were now staggering back into the clearing—many had been badly burned.

The only medicine available to treat their burns was the rendered-down fat from hippos which had been shot for food. A couple of the more sensible men were told to administer to the wounded, lathering the fat onto seared forearms, soles of feet and other extremities. In places the fire had melted the skin, leaving raw, bloodied meat that was starting to cook as the heat in the clearing reached unsurpassable temperatures.

The stiff wind driving the fire was blowing bits of burned grass forward into the clearing and my mind's concerns turned wholly to the possibility that one of these pieces would fall on a keg of gunpowder. One blade of burning grass on a keg is all it would take to blow up the entire clearing and all within it.

The fire had now all but encircled us. The smoke was no longer a dark vapour hanging in the air—it had taken on a solid consistency, at once turning the bright midday glare into an eerie twilight. Were it not for the noise, the shouting of orders, the screaming, you would have had the sense that you were alone, the person in front of you having dissolved into the smoke. The noise, accompanied by this feeling of isolation and the fire roaring—seemingly at your heels—brought with it the inevitable sense of terror and panic. Some of the slaves started to run blindly into the fire, to be immediately engulfed by a torrent of flames, their burning bodies emitting blood-curdling shrieks, further driving the spear of hysteria into the hearts and minds of those who remained in the clearing.

I could see that it would not take long for this madness to grip most of the party and swiftly issued the order for the guards to shoot anyone who started to panic and run. They were endangering me and affecting those who were able to think and act clearly. The shooting of a few slaves promptly sobered up the remainder of the party and I was able to regain control of the whole safari and put the slaves to work again.

Some animals came tearing into the clearing, their nostrils flaring, their eyes red and crazed. The guards immediately shot them, not allowing them to wreak any havoc. The meat would also go a long way in feeding the porters on our journey.

After quite some time we were able to get the better of the fire. It raged on, but had passed us.

The damage was assessed and we found that three porters were dead, burned beyond recognition. It was only when the others started to look around them, at those who were still alive, that we were able to ascertain who was dead. Six were injured, some by the fire itself, others by gunfire.

But thankfully all the goods were safe. A new problem now arose—how to distribute among the fit and living porters the goods that had been carried by the dead or injured. Goods were divided up, as evenly as possible, among the one hundred and ninety remaining slaves. Complaining was futile, and they knew it—all they would secure from such behaviour would be a harsh beating—their load would not be lightened. The *askaris* (soldiers, guards) forced the porters to fall in line and the journey continued.

Because of the fire and the time spent fighting it, it became obvious that we would not reach the village we were heading for, so I ordered the men to take a short cut to another village so that there would be no time lost.

The rest of the day was without incident, except for the tsetse flies. They were a terrible nuisance—buzzing around our mouths and biting our already sensitive skin. But my mind was not concerned with this. I was worried about the reception we would receive at the village, as it was not one commonly visited by safaris for the chief was not sympathetic with our style of business. It was not that he disagreed with the ownership of slaves, as he had many himself. It was more that he wished to be the owner of all slaves … to the exclusion of anyone else. Naturally he became jealous when he saw others—especially a safari of our size—with more slaves than he.

As we neared the village there was the usual announcement of our presence with our guns being fired, but it was evident as we drew nearer that we were not really welcome. Under such circumstances it was customary to be more vigilant and not enter the village oneself but to send in a senior guard with a couple of armed men—as a bodyguard—with presents and the request that the caravan be treated as friends. On this occasion it took considerable time for the advance guard to return, which in itself was worrying. It turned out that their delay was because of the avaricious demands made by the chief. His demeanour had changed dramatically when it was explained to him that a virtual army of men—all armed—waited close by.

In case of a trap the column advanced with caution. The porters were placed under a small guard while the rest went forward, guns at the ready—any indication of a trap would result in a fight.

As it turned out we were too early for the chief to set a trap. The number of armed men he had was small in comparison with those in my safari and they were visibly frightened at the prospect of having to take us on.

The chief ordered the villagers to produce many fowls, sheep and goats for the men of my safari as a sign of friendship, but as I had been forewarned of his slyness I demanded that all his men with guns be brought before me and lay down their arms. These were collected and put in a hut to be guarded by one of my sentries and one of his men, thus negating any treachery in his hospitality.

At first he protested a great deal, arguing that he had surely proved himself in the feast and offerings he had lain before us. While he gesticulated and feigned disbelief I quietly ordered some of my men to scout around the village to ensure that we were definitely not in any immediate danger of attack. As the discussions were nearing an end, a great deal of shouting and screaming jolted us, alerting our senses. The commotion was coming from behind us. The chief was noticeably embarrassed and it wasn't long before we understood why, although I'd had my suspicions.

A few of my best men were pushing two of his villagers—fully armed—in front of them, towards the chief's hut. They had hurriedly been posted on the outskirts of the village in the hope of getting a shot at me, in which case the chief would have been able to seize my safari. It was a matter of a couple of quick, curt orders and the chief was surrounded and held hostage until he could prove that he was worthy of his 'word' of friendship. The would-be assassins were then brought before me. Since we were short of porters they were forced into my gang and assigned loads that they would have to carry on the morrow.

All this appeared to shock the chief, who insistently professed his friendship, but I had been warned and my suspicions confirmed. These events were merely an indication to me that even greater precautions would have to be taken during the night. I took over a number of his huts for the night. In one, his son and daughter were placed as hostages. I felt sure he would not interfere again as long as their lives were in my hands. I was proved correct and the rest of the night was uneventful.

Before resting, the meat from the game that we had shot during the fire was salted and placed in strips on a platform of sticks over a low fire until it was dry. This prevented it from putrefying. The salt had been obtained from a place called Uvinza, many miles to the west, on the road to Ujiji, where there was a salt-water spring. Good salt was produced by boiling this water until it had completely evaporated. For years the people of Tanganyika had journeyed to the spring to collect water to make salt for themselves. The country in this area was barren and infested with tsetse fly, so no one lived there, yet many tracks had led to and from the spring in all directions. But it was no longer so—the Arabs had turned it into a business, making money from producing salt from the spring and selling it back to us.

The next morning discussions took place regarding payment for the food bought for the porters. On this occasion the payment was small as a result of the treatment that had been meted out to me—and at no extra cost we had acquired two of his villagers.

Our farewell was cold, with the sly chief feigning a cheerfulness of manner that quite failed to mask his bitterness. I ensured that my *askaris* watched our backs as the caravan snaked its way out of the village.

The distance that had to be covered on the fourth day was again long and arduous. The country we were entering offered a new set of challenges. There was no clear track on which to walk. Men had to walk in front of the column and hack a path for us with *pangas*, the heat did not relent and wild animals roamed this area in vast numbers. In a way this was to our advantage as we were always in need of food. A safari of our size—carrying such heavy loads—consumed enormous amounts of food. But untamed land with very few people and plenty of wild animals can also be a lethal combination.

During the day we shot plenty of buck as well as a buffalo. It was reported to me that a number of large elephants had been seen nearby at a point on the crossing of the Usenge plains. The lure of ivory decided me upon spending the night at this spot. It was already about two in the afternoon. We chose a shady area not far from water and made camp, taking the usual precautions to oversee the slaves and provide for the comforts of the *askaris*. As the decision was made to make camp instructions were issued to a couple of scouts to leave the party and pick up the spoor of the elephants. I stayed behind with some of my finest riflemen, preparing the guns. In due course one scout returned, reporting that the elephants were grazing in a thicket of acacia trees, about an hour's walk east of the camp. We set off immediately.

We were nearing the fullness of the hour predicted when we

heard a call well over to our right. It was the other scout. We headed in his direction and it was not long before we came across him, halfway up a tree. He looked up and pointed in front of him—the elephants were close. We could sense them through the dense bush. We would now have to exercise the utmost caution if we were to get close enough for a good shot at them without endangering our own lives.

We picked up the fresh spoor without much difficulty and were able to assess how close they were—ten, maybe twelve, yards. As we rounded a large anthill our estimations were confirmed as we saw the large mass of an elephant reaching high into an acacia, pulling vigorously at its branches. We were downwind and, for that moment, had the advantage. The elephant moved slightly, reaching toward another branch outside of the undergrowth and was immediately in profile. He had the most magnificent tusks—this bull was no youngster—his tusks were long and with a sizeable girth. An old battle scar, a tussle over a cow in season or a more serious clash with another bull for control of the herd perhaps, ran the length of his left flank. Dry, cracked mud caked his back.

There were nine guns including mine, each loaded with heavy charges of seven fingers of powder and three-ounce balls. I whispered, barely audibly, that we were all to fire at the bull at the same time. No sooner had I uttered these words than another elephant came into sight. Quickly, hurriedly, I changed the instructions. Four guns were to fire at the second elephant, while the others and I would shoot the big bull.

We were lying low in the undergrowth. I held my breath while those who needed to shift themselves into a good firing position did so, hoping they would not accidentally move too suddenly or make a noise. We were in position. I breathed out, preparing to shoot first. The big bull stood only eight yards from me, broadside on. Taking careful aim at his heart, I fired. No sooner had my gunpowder exploded than the others fired. The cloud of gunpowder smoke was thick before us, making visibility difficult. We would not be able to ascertain whether we'd hit our respective marks until the smoke cleared. This was the most anxious time. There is nothing more dangerous than a wounded elephant. Time stood still, the acrid smell of the gunpowder stinging our noses. Every fibre, every muscle, every sense paused to listen. Our shots would undoubtedly have alerted the other elephants, raising the alarm. The sound of gunfire in these remote parts is foreign to animals, their reactions thus irrational and dangerous. At any moment the rest of the herd was liable to charge, but in which direction? Instinctively we lay flat on the ground, reloading our guns as quickly and as quietly as we could.

Just then the smoke cleared. I saw no results of our shooting. This was not unusual though, as the elephants, having been mortally wounded would have stampeded off. We picked up their spoor quite easily and, after tracking it for about two hundred yards, came across the big bull, still standing, but swaying slightly from side to side. Although very near to death he was still extremely dangerous. He scented us immediately and swung to face us, screaming, ears flapping. There is no more frightening noise than that of an elephant about to charge. The screams penetrate one's soul, terrifying screams that grip your gut and twist your nerve.

We fired our guns as one, killing the old bull where he stood.

The other elephant was nowhere to be seen and quite possibly the shots we had just fired had frightened it off even farther away. I stayed behind with three of the men to cut out the massive tusks while the others went off after the second elephant. We were busy with the bloody business of chopping up the dead bull's skull to get to the tusks when much shouting and shooting was heard some distance away. The small party had obviously found the second elephant. Then silence.

Suddenly two men came thrashing through the undergrowth, the fear gripping their bellies evident on their faces—they had clearly been chased and we grabbed our weapons, preparing for the worst.

We soon learned that the crazed animal, wild with pain and fury, had doubled-back and caught the trackers unaware from behind. The erratic shots and shouting had been as a result of this surprise attack by the elephant. The news was grave—it was possible that some of the men had been hurt, even killed.

The ashen-faced men led the way, fingers at the trigger, their bodies twitching with nervous anticipation—yet they moved with the stealth and agility of animals themselves. The sight of the confrontation was clear—trees had been trampled, branches hung limp from the trunks of bigger trees, but nothing else—just blood and a pregnant silence.

The men were alive, shaken but safe, hiding a little way off. Carefully and soundlessly we searched for the spoor we knew had to be there. A scout to my left, himself a worthy rifleman, picked it up. The imprint from the front leg was deep and blood had pooled in the impression it had made on the dry ground. Not yet dry in the earth, we knew the elephant couldn't be far off.

Minutes after picking up the spoor, the piercing scream struck us and we readied ourselves for the charge that we surely knew would come. A blind crashing through trees indicated the direction whence the animal lunged. We were spread out into a half-moon shape, a few yards apart, when the elephant burst into sight, pain no longer registering. Riddled with bullets, the animal's only instinct was to flee, but anger denied it the luxury of measured judgment. There was a thunderous roar as the guns went off. When the smoke cleared the elephant lay before us, struggling with consciousness, still screaming in pain and rage and fear.

Three further shots from the best guns silenced it, forever.

The ivory was cut from the heads of the two beasts and tracks were made back to camp, but not before the appropriate ceremonies had been performed over the corpses of the dead elephants.

A special kind of grass in the area, called *kaleza*, was gathered, bundled and burned, driving the spirits away. When the tusks were cut out the nerves were exposed with great care, visible only to the person doing the cutting. From the nerves two bracelets would be cut and worn on the wrists of those who possessed the strength to harness their magic. These bracelets held the power to have a person killed by the spirit of the dead elephant. A special medicine had already been prepared for this person, for this occasion. These rituals prevented the spirits of the dead animal returning to seek its vengeance. The nerve bracelets would become hard and looked much like the ivory from which they had been taken.

Our return took no longer than an hour. On nearing the camp, we announced our homecoming, firing our guns. There was much whistling so that the second-in-command of the safari could meet our small hunting party and bestow honour on the leader. When we arrived at camp there was great rejoicing by all. My hands were lifted up to great ululation to show that it was I who had truly defeated the elephants through wisdom and courage. The tusks were laid down in front of my tent so that all could see the value I had obtained on this day. Many of the porters asked if they could go out and collect some of the meat that had been left behind. It was immediately arranged that thirty men with armed guards would go to the dead elephants and bring back as much meat as could be carried.

On arriving they were put through a ritual so that none would acquire the strength and power or the wisdom of the elephants. They approached the dead animals from below wind, holding grass firebrands in their hands, waving them over their heads and then sweeping them to the ground, chanting in unison:

Oh mighty beast of all,
Oh mighty animal of all the forest,
With the greatest strength and wisdom of all wild creatures,
Thou hast fallen to the wise.
Allah be praised.

A special fire was then lit at each animal's head and tail, blowing smoke over the entire body. Only the leader of the party could approach to see if the spirits had departed. All the while the chanting was kept up to drive away the evil spirits. Then many hundreds of pounds of meat were hacked off and neatly stacked nearby, caution being taken that the stomach was not punctured—as this would let out the greatest of all evils. No one had lived in sanity who had punctured the stomach of a dead elephant without first having chewed the leaves of *sonkora*, spitting the pulp on the elephant's anus and throat before closing his eyes so that naught could be seen by the spirits of the dead animal.

When as much meat as could be carried had been cut, it was evenly distributed among the men who then headed back to camp where they would begin cutting it into strips, salting it and hanging it on poles to dry over a fire. By morning it would be dry and added to the loads already carried by the slaves. But it was not the food of Islam and thus some cloven-hoofed animals had to be shot for meat for the believers.

The next day the safari struck out again with the usual complaints from the porters. No notice was taken of them though, as they had to carry their loads whether they liked it or not.

It was late in the day when we arrived at the village of Uriwira—to be greeted with uncertainty and suspicion. We did not pay much heed as we were the masters of the area. Any village that did not respect our wishes or threatened us in any way would simply be pillaged and burned to the ground. Those not shot or mutilated would be our slaves for life. We were now nearing the area of great profit and wealth—villages in which could be found many desirable girls of young age, boys who would make good strong slaves and men who would make good porters once trained into obedience.

There were two days left of the safari before we would reach the area where the real trading would begin. These two days proved to be the most gruelling of our trip—there was much to be negotiated. The area was populated with warring nomads, those who had been driven from their villages—reasons varied from theft to taking another man's wife. They wandered the country, pillaging, living on what they could take by force. My guards had to be at their most vigilant—these wild vagrants were usually armed and always considered dangerous. Isolation and starvation could drive a man to many a sin. At times we would see one a way off and managed to defuse the situation without too much ado. But at other times, seemingly from nowhere a ragged, corpse-like face would appear in front of us or amidst the gang of porters. These nomads emanated a fearlessness born from desolation— they welcomed death and thus did not fear it, making them all the more dangerous.

Human savages were not the only problem—this far west the bush teemed with wild and equally dangerous animals. Once, I remember, we had all retired to our beds for the night when a cry, so tormented and agonized that it made your skin crawl, rose into the night. A hyena had wandered into the camp and removed the face of one of the porters. There was nothing that could be done for the man except bathe his face with water as hot as he could stand and then pour oil, collected from the joints of an elephant's legs, onto the gaping wound that was his face. The oil was of great value for many things as it did not dry but remained sticky and thus adhered to the wound. Guards were placed so that no further incidents of this nature would happen again.

The next day the man had to be carried lying in a blanket, strapped to a pole in the form of a *mashila*. He would be left at the next village to recover from his wounds or die, depending on the wishes of Allah. When evening drew near he was in great pain and found it difficult to eat or drink. What remained of his face was a swollen, bloodied, purple mess of flesh and oozing pus.

But then, many had suffered the same fate and survived.

At this last stop we knew that on the morrow we would come across our first proper trading village and therefore had to proceed with extra caution so as not to give away the slightest hint of our imminent arrival. To give away our position might mean the disappearance of valuable trading items. The night was spent in comfort except that the de-faced man moaned for comfort and we could give him little.

The guns were checked and made ready. The goods for barter were counted and recounted so that my exact wealth with which to trade was known, as well as the value of the ivory we were carrying, which was of great value in Zanzibar.

All were called to prayer and the last praises to Allah were made.

"Ila ilaha ila Allah."

"There is only one God and that is God."

It was a command, not a request, for all to pray. The heathens had to pray to God and learn the Koran.

III

The morning broke with the usual awakening of birds singing in the trees, the cackle of guinea fowl and the distant hoot of the great hornbills announcing their hunger. Lions roared to denote a satisfactory night's feast and human sounds hummed around the embers of dying fires.

Our first target village was only a few hours' walk away so absolute silence had to be maintained. Our safari was divided into three groups—an advance scouting party that preceded us by an hour, followed by the main fighting body, then the porters and the sick—all of whom, except the victim of the hyena attack, had to walk—bringing up the rear. The tension in the air was thick. There were no illusions that the morning could quite possibly develop into a gun battle. It was clear that silent prayers were being offered that there would simply be an enemy surrender.

The only ones to benefit from the booty we had travelled so far to take would, of course, be my soldiers and me. The slaves would merely be allowed to look upon the scene; perhaps with memories flooding back of the day they had been so coldly uprooted from their own families, from their own liberty.

The sun was up about three hours when the scouts came back to report that the village was going about its daily work in a normal way. There appeared to be no suspicion that a raid was about to take place. It was reported that, aside from some gardens on the eastern side of the village where some form of activity was taking place—probably because of the coming rainy season—all the inhabitants were in the village.

This was the moment when I would truly prove myself to be a man of wealth, a man to be respected. I had planned my strategy carefully. In the fourth hour of the sun the village came into sight. Under cover of the virtually impenetrable bush, five men were to move around the garden, five were to head to the west of the village and another five to the north to block potential escape routes. The remainder, about twelve of us, would move into the village from the south. Sufficient time would be given for the men to get into place and then two guns would be fired, officially signifying the start of the raid. Four guns would be fired when the operation was over. The porters would remain, under escort, about half a mile away to await further instructions. Care was taken to ensure that all movements were made noiselessly so as not to lose the element of surprise.

This tribe was completely unpredictable. At times they were known to have fought but at others to submit with no resistance, thus all the precautions.

All guns were loaded and ready.

The order was given to move into position. Should there be the slightest indication that the village was aware of our presence, we were to charge and capture all who could be seen, irrespective of age or size. Sorting out the spoils would be done later, when either bartering with the chief or simply ordering him to do as told.

After a while there was a shout from the southern side, indicating that our movements had been spotted. A villager had immediately raised the alarm, sending a wave of panic through the village with men, women and children running in all directions, hoping to escape the raid.

It was all in vain. My men moved in swiftly and simultaneously. Only a few arrows were unleashed at the raiding party. We returned fire with our muzzle-loaders. This was unnecessary as the villagers had never intended to fight but the initial panic had caused some confusion.

Soon the village was surrounded and the terrified villagers brought under my control. They were made to congregate in the central meeting area. The chief was brought before me and forced to lay down his weapons at my feet—symbolic of his surrender and his subservience. He was not an old man but seemed weak-willed. By contrast, his captain was a man of great strength and determination and no doubt it was because of him that the tribe had gained its powerful reputation. But since they had all been taken by such surprise there was not a thing any one of them could have done.

The chief came forward and, in an effort to save face with his people, made an attempt to dignify himself.

"This day has never before been seen in this village of mine. Had my scouts been awake this would never have happened to me and my people. Because I have my guns laid in front of me I can only say that I must do what I am bid, or risk having the village destroyed which would not be for the good of my people. I must ask you to speak to me on equal terms since it was only like a jackal that you have captured my village, and not like a man. What do you come for? What do you ask of me?"

The answer was easy.

"Look at what I have brought and at the number of men I have with me. First I must tell you to call all your warriors before me to lay down their weapons. Only then can we talk as great men. If this is not done I will order my men to forcibly disarm your men. This is not as great people should meet and talk."

The chief indicated to his people that my instructions were to be carried out. One by one his warriors came before me and laid their weapons in the dust at my feet. His captain, a tall, muscular man as black at the night sky before the coming of the new moon, was last to perform this task, clearly at odds with his conscience and his pride. The risk of defiance, however, was too great and he placed his gun on the ground, never once lifting his gaze directly from the eyes of my own captain. Looking at me in this manner would have caused him serious trouble and might even have cost him his life.

I was in charge—a man of wealth, a man to be revered. I was now the master of this village and its people, the slaves to be.

The weapons were immediately removed by my own guards to a safe distance behind me and placed under close watch—so that none might suddenly rush forward and grab one of these crudely shaped yet lethal weapons and kill me.

I was standing facing the chief, my back towards the southern entrance. For just the briefest moment—before he was able to catch himself and regain his composure—I noticed a look of unguarded delight and greed cross the chief's face as the porters arrived with our goods for barter. The goods were laid out and there was now no doubt that the chief would co-operate. Not even for sake of appearance did he make a show of being a hard bargainer, much to the visible distaste of his captain and to a lesser degree his people, the very people he was entrusted to protect. His eyes lit up at the bales of silk. He ran his podgy fingers through bowls of beads, ready to trade a life for a new robe, a new headdress, a mirror in which to stare at his own reflection.

My next request was that all the maidens in the village be brought before me so that a selection of the most desirable ones could be made. Some came forward defiantly, others hesitantly and some, mostly the younger girls, clung to the legs of their mothers. Although too young to fully understand, perhaps they had a sense of their own impending fate. Few of the girls were clothed, and a good many pleasing to look upon. Those ranging in age from about eight years to puberty were first to be scrutinized. In total there must have been about sixty of them. The very thin ones were first to be sorted out. They were not completely dismissed—on closer investigation some might prove useful, though in the main they did not have what it would take to make the arduous journey back and would, in any case, not fetch a good price on the slave markets of Zanzibar and Dar es Salaam.

There was no question of entertaining emotion in the business of slave-trading. One had to pay attention to physical characteristics only, to divorce oneself from the low wailing of the village wives, their daughters' fates in the hands of a stranger. For me this was purely business and I found myself unaffected, even as one woman fell to the dust, begging for the life of her sickly child. The girls who had reached puberty were also separated as there was little chance of them still being virgins, which in business meant a difference in price.

The others were then examined.

First their hair, to see that it was not patchy or sparsely grown—an indication that they were not of good blood. Then their faces and teeth were inspected. They were made to open their mouths wide and with a stick their lips, teeth and tongue were probed so that any defect could be seen. If they had breasts they had to be examined for scars on account of tribal origin. The same applied to their stomachs. Their hips and groins had to be of good proportion, their legs shapely and strong. Their breasts had to show fertility and satisfaction. The younger girls who had not reached the change to puberty were checked for their apparent sturdiness and their future development carefully judged.

The girls were thus sorted and made to stand in ranks of varying grades. Throughout this process my guards helped maintain order and control. Desperate mothers had to be kept away and where possible, silenced. It upset the girls to hear their mothers wailing and screaming and this made it the more difficult to maintain order. The youths and boys were then called to the fore and were grouped in their various ages of maturity. They were made to strip completely naked so as to better determine their age and, of course, their standard of physique. They varied in age from about six years to near-manhood. They were sorted according to their stamina, development and appearance of strength. Some would be made eunuchs, others slaves and others porters.

After this detailed examination of the youth of the village, the intense business of bartering for their lives got underway. Bales of cloth were produced, beads, bangles, mirrors and many other minor items. A price for each person had to be established and the appropriate family member negotiated with. One villager was particularly difficult. He valued his son greatly and did not want to part with him but, because he was a fine-looking young man of great strength and would undoubtedly fetch a high price on the slave market, he was of great value to me as well. Two bales of cloth, four mirrors, six wire loops of beads and a keg of gunpowder was the price eventually settled upon.

Next was a boy of about ten who looked as though he might be of use, although he was rather thin and had front teeth that had been filled. In payment I had to consider he would in future be of some expense to his buyer and thus he was bought cheaply, though not without considerable argument.

Some of the girls were equally expensive but there were also those blemished by nature or custom who fetched much cheaper prices.

The total paid out for the slaves bought that day was forty bales of cloth, thirty bundles of wire for making bangles, ten boxes of beads and eight kegs of gunpowder. The village was not rich, however, and what little ivory they did have I took as payment for the trouble the chief had caused.

Specially selected huts were demanded of the chief. The heavily guarded slaves were then herded into the huts and bound with heavy ropes and sticks to prevent them from running away.

Of course the girls had been selected for a very different purpose from the men and some of them were thus allowed more freedom to perform the tasks for which they were now destined. The men were allowed out only to relieve themselves and this only under armed guard. It was made perfectly clear, and was by no means an empty threat, that should they try to escape my guards would shoot to kill without warning—and that the value of the goods exchanged for that slave would immediately have to be reimbursed.

During the night there was much wailing and steady sobbing from the huts in which the younger boys and girls were being held. They were too young to understand what had happened that day—too young to know that they would never grow up to experience the freedom and kinship of their village—too young to know that some of them might be sold at the Dar es Salaam slave market only to be shipped to faraway lands, perhaps never to walk on their native soil again—too young to realize that in a few days we would leave and some would not make the journey to Tabora. All they knew at that moment was that they felt alone and scared. They had been prodded and poked all day, bartered for and purchased for a few strings of beads and a bale of cloth.

I knew—from experience—that this bereavement would only last a day or two. Then they would usually give over to their fates, let it lead them to whatever life it had in store for them. Slavery was a fact of life and villagers lived with the knowledge that one day it might be their lot.

The next day the slaves who had accompanied me thus far on the safari were sent into the bush to cut forked sticks about three feet long. The new slaves would be yoked to these sticks—by their necks— and then in turn tied to each other. This would prevent any opportunists from trying to run away during the long journey that lay ahead.

In all we had made eighty purchases, among these some adult men, and about twenty tusks of ivory, which had cost me nothing but would fetch a good price in Zanzibar.

Day broke and many of the villagers were already standing outside their huts, waiting to see their loved ones move off on their way to permanent captivity. Of the captives, most of the older ones seemed to have accepted their fate and stood stoically in the bright light of the morning while their feet were being shackled. Most of the younger ones seemed to have exhausted their tears during the night, staring vacantly ahead or being gently consoled by others only slightly older than they. They did not think, they did not believe—they only stared—until it was time to move on. Overnight this had become a ghost village, devoid of emotion, its life milked and left to cake in the dust.

There was always some confusion when it came time to leave. Who would look after the slaves? In what order would the safari march? After much jostling and shouting and distributing loads among the new slaves, the entire party was eventually lined up, awaiting the order to march. Only I could give the order.

At about eight o'clock I was satisfied that the safari was ready to proceed. I barked the order and slowly, feet shuffling, hindered by rope and spirit, the caravan lurched forward.

The remaining villagers tried to catch a final glimpse of their loved ones, recognizing many but helpless as the train edged past. It would be the last time they would see their beloved sons, daughters, friends, husbands.

This departure would not be marked with singing and chanting. No guns would be fired to signify our withdrawal, no small children running alongside the safari, laughing and playing, waving at us. No, not this time—just the hot sting of angry eyes on our backs as we walked away.

The safari had swelled to about three hundred in total—a long line of burdened humanity, not knowing where they were going or where they would be living out their days or, in fact, in what manner—expressionless faces wondering if and when they might receive a meal.

After having trudged for about two hours, a rest was called to decide whether a further raid on another village might be desirable or if the party should return to Tabora. It was decided that some of the slaves would return under escort to Tabora while others would continue west to Lake Tanganyika, where ivory could be purchased and possibly more slaves.

So it was that when we arrived at Nkonde village with a show of strength, we were given all assistance that could be afforded to a safari of such a nature, and the party was divided into two.

In this foreign place, away from their families for the first time, there was much crying at night but it was made clear by a few severe beatings that this behaviour would not be tolerated. After a few unfortunates had been made examples, the sobs dried up. The older slaves who had more of an understanding of what had happened provided comfort to the younger children, encouraging them to sleep, for they would need their strength in the days to come. No one was allowed to leave the party without either my or my senior captain's permission, and then, only under escort.

Slaves were money and therefore valuable.

My senior guards and I made use of the younger girls during the nights. Although virgins, they had been trained from a young age as to what a woman's duties were to a man. They gave themselves with comfort and satisfaction, knowing that this would afford them privileges for the duration of the safari, and certainly more freedom than the rest. They had nothing to lose—this was to be their new life and nothing else mattered. If they fell pregnant the fathers would assume responsibility for them and their children for the rest of their lives. At least this was tangible, known.

Thus it was that Saidi bin Sheriff was sent back to Tabora with one hundred and fifty slaves of all sizes and ages, to be handed over to my father—the fruits of my first slave-raid. The rest of us were to continue to Lake Tanganyika to see what other business could be found and what greater profits might be acquired. My decision to split the party and continue to the lake was not based solely on commercial gain. I had dreamed many a night of the wonders of the lake and had heard much spoken thereof—I longed to see it for myself, to witness its splendour.

IV

The safari to Lake Tanganyika was not as eventful as the first part of the expedition. We passed a number of villages that had been burned to the ground, obviously raided before our arrival. For the most part they were devoid of life. Here and there a lone chicken picked through the charred remains of what was once the village maize field. At a couple of these villages a few old men and women, hunched and painfully thin, wandered around, seemingly aimlessly, scraping together a meagre existence. In terror they would watch our approach from a distance, the recent horrors still too vivid in their minds to trust such a large party of strangers.

Others seemed unaffected by our presence, as though too much had been taken from them to care. At one such village my captain approached an old woman, stooped low, going about much the same business as her chickens. Stooped before him she looked up, shielding her eyes from the midday glare, too weary or too bitter to straighten and meet his gaze. She didn't so much speak as spit words at him—her contempt for him, for me, for our entire party, for what we represented, in her every syllable. She gave no details, but it was not detail we were after. We had no interest in how events had played out or why the village had been burned. From her we learned that a slave-raiding party had passed through three days prior and were headed towards Lake Tanganyika via Ilumbie's village. It had been my intention to travel that way, but on hearing this I decided to swing in a more southerly direction toward Rungwa and thence west to the great lake.

The first village we came across took me somewhat by surprise after the chaos and hostility of the previous village we had raided. Nothing could have been more different. The villagers simply stood around, made no effort to run or defend themselves and the chief offered no resistance. We could take our pick of whatever we wanted at very little cost. It seemed to me the chief was well aware that a far greater cost was attached to resisting a raiding party. Perhaps he had first-hand experience or had heard it told.

His people had been forewarned and, though they feigned calm and resignation, their eyes told a different story. But I had no interest in their fears. It was not dignified to concern myself with such trivia—all that mattered was how easy the chief had made things for us.

We were able to obtain a number of young men, boys and girls. Most of them would be used to carry the loads that various porters, after their onerous journey, were no longer physically capable of carrying. The rest were tethered together.

The area was well populated with game, good for food but also for the tsetse flies that were proving to be more and more of a nuisance. Their constant buzzing around our heads, gathering at the corners of our mouths and eyes, was irritating in the extreme. Their bites were sore and lethal. Valuable porters fell prey to the deadly sleeping sickness. Although it might take some years to die from this insidious disease the painful red swellings from the bites quickly developed into the inevitable fever and drowsiness, rendering them useless as porters.

For this reason slaves were furnished with giraffe tails to swish around the heads and bodies of the more important persons in the safari. Misuse of a swat led to dire consequences. Punishments were based on the value of the offender, but in the main harsh beatings were administered, always in full view of the others—to dissuade those who may have been harbouring similar thoughts.

Wild honey was plentiful as well as food from the raided villages. Ivory could be bought in large quantities. More slaves had to be acquired to carry the increasing amount of ivory as well as additional food for the ever-growing safari.

After two weeks of travelling and raiding, there it was—Lake Tanganyika. No stories, no matter how vivid, how detailed, could have prepared me for, or have even come close to, the reality. I had heard that when standing on the sandy banks you could stare all the way to where the land fell away into itself and not see its end, and this was true, no matter in which direction you looked.

I found myself deeply moved.

A great deal of shouting and singing spontaneously rose up from the several-hundred-strong safari, chanting praises to the lake, to Allah and to me. This was a turning point in our journey and signified our return to Tabora.

I would return to the lake many times in my life and be awed each time, but never would this first stirring that it aroused in me move me in quite the same way.

There were three villages near the lakeshore but they had had frequent demands made on them in the past and had converted to Islam for protection. From these villages we were able to gain valuable information concerning other villages that had not been raided in recent times. We would use the village of Karema as our base for a few days while we carried out raids on the untouched villages. Our purchases would now extend from slaves and ivory to rhino horn, hippo hides and other things useful for sale to the traders in Zanzibar.

The slaves were put to building a *boma* to house them. This they had to do while harnessed together—they had cost a lot and could not be lost through carelessness.

The first few days were used to check and count our supplies, the guns were cleaned and gunpowder and percussion balls laid in the sun to dry so they would not let us down by misfiring.

It took two days to prepare for what would become our final raid. The village was taken completely by surprise and had little chance to retaliate. The raid unfolded in its usual manner—hysteria bordering on madness sweeping through the people—but they had nowhere to run and, in many cases, when panic gave way to clarity, most accepted their fate philosophically—as merely one of those things that happens to a person in this life.

This was true of those times.

The trading had been so good that there was little left for us with which to barter and I decided not to proceed to another village. We spent the rest of the day making arrangements to return to Karema. The trip took three days, with the slaves always slowing the pace, not to mention the vast bulk we were now carrying. On nearing Karema a great jubilation went up from the men who had stayed behind, as well as from the people of the village, who realized that no further demands would be made of them.

The following day was used for rest and prayer to Mohammed—He who had made the safari so profitable. Some of the slaves were introduced to the religion of Islam and were forced to perform prayers although they had little idea of what they were doing. In time, however, they would understand and receive the teachings of Mohammed in full, though only after circumcision.

V

On the morning of the fourth day, after laborious preparations, the return trip to Tabora began. Villagers slunk out of their huts to watch us leave. Under the surface of contrived joviality that accompanied our departure ran a deep vein of relief.

In single file, neck-to-neck, the slaves needed little reminder that they were no longer free—no longer free the make their own choices or survey their land with a light heart.

Askaris walked alongside the long line of men, women and children, encouraging them to greater effort. Full discipline had not yet been established and obedience was often only achieved with whips.

Each evening, allowing enough time before dark, the slaves would be herded together, some being called upon to cut brushwood and poles to construct a *boma* for them and other members of the retinue. Cooking would then begin. Needless to say this was a massive task, there now being some one hundred and fifty slaves, one hundred porters and the *askaris*.

Prayers were called just before sunset—all work was stopped and heads turned toward the east while I chanted the prayers. After each prayer everyone had to bow in the manner of Islam. Confused slaves copied those who knew what they were doing.

Those who did not obey, whether out of ignorance or obstinacy, were severely dealt with as it was considered sacrilegious not to follow all that Mohammed had taught. In time they would have to embrace the true belief of Islam so I considered this good training.

Since water was a long walk from where we were currently encamped, we made an early start after morning prayers on the second day.

During the course of the day, head counts were frequently undertaken. After one such count an *askari* reported to me that two slaves were missing. Infuriated, I called an immediate halt. Not only did this waste valuable time but also might inspire others to do the same, not to mention the fact that they had cost me dearly.

A handful of carefully picked *askaris* were sent in different directions to locate the missing slaves. Their double-sided, forked-neck sticks would impede their progress. Soon enough two young men, fine-looking and strong—thus costly—were found hiding in the nearby scrub.

With much screaming, kicking and the occasional crack of a whip the two offenders were brought before me on their hands and knees. Fear now folded into their contempt and earlier bravado. It was necessary for me to hand down a punishment that would not only break their spirit and force them to acquiesce to their new lot but would also be enough of a lesson from which the others might learn. Publicly they were stripped of their scant clothing and, with hippo-hide whips, flogged for all to bear witness.

Their anguished cries, as each crack came down on their naked skin, pierced the air, raw and voluminous at first but fading into a low, sapped moaning. The rest of the slaves stood watching, staring at the spectacle, perceptibly drawing back with each crack, each cry. The two young men were not the only ones being broken—all the older slaves knew this to be a warning and would thus heed it, letting go of their last fragile grip on their will. The two slaves were beaten until they lay crumpled in the dirt, their blood running freely, their spirits draining into the dry bush.

The smaller children were beginning to cry again, but it was no longer necessary for my men to intercede and discipline them— their peers now hushed them.

There was no time to waste. Once the flogging was done with, the men were made to stand and then tied to another four slaves, making it impossible to escape.

Toward the end of the day we reached the forest and with it the promise of water. After the debilitating heat of the day and the intolerable tsetse fly the cool canopy of the forest was a welcome reprieve. Being the leader of the safari I, however, did not have as rough a time of it. I had slaves dedicated to tending my every need.

That night a shattering cry sliced through the blackness of the night. The violence of the cry had such a recklessness to it that the entire camp was simultaneously awake, jolted from sleep and swung off balance. The source was traced through the uneasiness spreading among the slaves. Torches were lit in time to see a lion, its amber eyes glinting in the light, dragging off a young slave. Fuelled by fear the victim fought his executioner, his pain manifesting itself through terrified screams, alternating with guttural sounds of anguish emanating from his hideously contorted face.

The lion had now disappeared behind the *boma* wall but the legs of his prey were still visible, twitching, dragging in the dirt. Shots were fired into the vicinity of the attack but it was impossible to tell whether any had found their mark.

An eerie silence descended on both the camp and its surrounds, collective breaths held, straining for the slightest sound—only seconds later to be broken by the agonized wailing of the slaves close enough to hear the satisfied grunting and mauling as the lion's canines ripped through lifeless flesh.

Fires were lit and more guards posted in case the intruder returned. A head count was done and it was found that two were missing, but we could not tell whether both had fallen victim to wild beasts or had merely used the ensuing chaos as an opportunity to escape.

As first light forced the night sky into retreat we were able to see that both the missing persons had been savaged by lions. Stealth and surprise on their side, the lions had approached the encampment and found easy prey. One victim had been taken headfirst and was thus not able to scream, while the other, waking us, had been dragged off by his shoulder.

Two of the *askaris* were ordered to follow the spoor and to recover the bodies or parts thereof. After a while they returned with only bits of flesh and pieces of cloth. One carried a bloodied hand and an unidentifiable lump of caked flesh. The lions had had a good meal.

It was our intention to stop at Rungwa village on the third night, having forced a hard day's march. A further five days remained before reaching Tabora. At this Islamic village we would be able to take proper prayers and give thanks for our good fortunes. The stop was uneventful. The chief bought one of the slaves from me, a good-looking, strong young man worthy of thirty tusks of ivory, six rhino horns and twenty giraffe tails—a good price considering the great distance from Dar es Salaam and Zanzibar.

During the course of the fourth day it became necessary to do away with some of the slaves—those who had become too sick or too weak to continue the journey and who would thus fetch no price at the market. They were herded into the nearby bush and clubbed over the head. To ensure they did not survive their legs were also broken, leaving them for the hyenas at nightfall. This was done out of view but close enough for us to hear the sharp thud as club met skull. When the *askaris* returned, the order to continue was given. The reality of the event sunk in and those entertaining thoughts of malingering soon abandoned such ideas.

The safari proceeded on its way to Tabora where we were due to arrive the following day. There was great excitement among my retinue in anticipation of seeing their loved ones, even though there had been no shortage of girls from the time of the first slave raid. Some girls had already been chosen as concubines by the *askaris*. I too, though still young, had chosen two girls who were only about twelve years old but showed signs of great fertility.

We made an early start the following day so as not to make a late arrival in Tabora. The atmosphere was divided, apprehension and renewed fear coursing through the slaves and jubilation lightening the hearts and step of those returning home.

In the afternoon we caught our first glimpse of smoke from the evening cooking fires curling up from the roofs of the huts. We knew we were on the outskirts of Unyanyembe and Tabora. Cultivated gardens came into view, spreading out among the huts, and with each new sighting of home our excitement mounted, shrouding the nervous anticipation the slaves were experiencing. Some of the *askaris* fired their guns, alerting the villagers of our arrival. The final two miles to Tabora were across open savannah and it was not long before the first children came running to meet us.

My parents knew it was I, Ali, returning from my first safari.

Men were shouting greetings, children were squealing with delight, running next to their fathers and brothers, totally caught up in the moment. Our entrance to the village was soon paved with a mass of singing, dancing women—praising Allah for our safe return—children, little hands grabbing onto their fathers', would every now and then join the singing, shouting choruses.

And there, at the end of it all, my father, his face glowing with pride, my mother at his side. He ordered the slaughter of a number of goats and other delicacies and it was not long before the cooking fires were exuding the familiar flavours of home through the effervescent chatter of bustling women.

VI

My reception on arriving home is a difficult one to describe—
there was so much to tell, so many stories, so much news to catch
up on. During the feast everyone spoke at once, each wanting to
tell his story in greater detail and with more licence than the next.
Singing and dancing ignited the still night air, with the constant
rhythm of hand-clapping and feet thumping the dry earth
adding such a vigorous dimension to the affair that the feasting
and celebrations continued through the night and well into the
following day. But not before, when the sun hung suspended in
the western sky, prayers were held. Allah was thanked for the safe
return of his son who had proved he was no longer a boy and no
longer needed to be cared for by his parents.

Although the feasting marked my successful return it was also
to some extent a celebration of my coming of age. I had returned
from my first safari that I alone had led—the first slaving and
trading expedition from which I had profited. I had become a
man and was recognized as such.

It was a great day for me.

From that day on I had my own slaves to tend to my needs, as
a man. My first proper wife had already been chosen for me from
a noble family of my father's tribe. The concubines I had taken

as my own on the raid would bear my offspring but none would be afforded the respect and privilege due to the children born of a proper wife.

The slaves were divided—men and women, older and younger. Each group was interned in a secure *boma* and allowed time to rest and recuperate from the journey. They were fed well and frequently inspected for disease, their health and vitality critical to their re-sale.

After falling into an exhausted sleep, I woke to the now-familiar sounds of the feast recommencing. The festivities broke with a renewed robustness, during which time the finer girls captured during the trip were brought before us, with all their beauty, suppleness and agility on display. Their bodies were lithe and perfect in every respect, their firm breasts rounded and pert, moving as one with their vibrating chests. The muscles on their buttocks rippled as they danced. Their varied complexions were without blemish, smooth and aglow in the orange radiance of the fires. Each movement highlighted some new characteristic—a face in profile, a strong, shapely leg. Their dance was alternately measured and provocative, building in tempo to crescendos that demonstrated their dancing abilities and endurance. At its most frenetic the stomping and shaking, dipping and spinning would ebb into a low, pulsating fluidity. The wealthy onlookers gazed in wanton admiration. Prices were offered and in some cases the tender acquired from such sales was most handsome.

Three days later the festivities gave way to hard work. The slaves I had bought had been fed and given ample time to rest. It was time now to re-examine and prepare them for market. We used the same criteria as that of the raid, but this time the process was far more critical for we were no longer buying, but selling.

First the older men were paraded and graded—they would be sold as common labour to work in fields, tend livestock and perform other such menial tasks. The women were similarly checked, except that additional points were noted—whether they'd had children or not, whether they'd be suitable as concubines, or whether they were only fit for use as chamber maids to look after the wives of the buyers. It was important to note who was related to whom, so that slaves would not live together with their relatives.

We then moved on to the younger men and boys. The most notable distinction here was whether or not they had reached puberty and, if not, how long it would be before they did. From this inspection it was decided which were suitable to become eunuchs—mostly children between the ages of five and eight were earmarked for this. All had to be circumcised in accordance with the teachings of Islam. The girls were checked for virginity and physical development. Little girls would mostly be brought up to become attendants to wives and concubines.

Most importantly all slaves had to be initiated into the belief of Islam. All had to learn the prayers and teachings of Mohammed— simple enough for the girls, who were also taught how to cook and behave in the appropriate Islamic manner and how to conduct themselves when called upon by a man or a future owner.

Things were a lot more gruelling for the boys as a result of their requisite circumcisions, not to mention the operations that had to be performed on those selected to become eunuchs.

A special grass enclosure had been built and would be used as both a school and an operating area. The great day came for all males to be operated upon—a day that would bring them into the religion of Islam as true and full believers. Lined up outside the enclosure were special drummers whose duty it was to beat the drums with a certain timing and tone—in order to drown out the cries from within so that those awaiting the operation would not hear. The first youth was brought in for the *nganga* to perform the rite according to Islamic law. An ordinary knife was used and there was no anaesthetic.

The boy's eyes were wide with fright and his breathing came in short, raspy gasps, his muscles taut with nervousness and anticipation. His attempts at bravery imploded with the flesh sliced from his manhood. After his initial screams the sound emanating from him became more animal-like, a low, haunted grunting. Weak and disorientated he was ushered into an adjoining camp to recover. For him the vigorous drum-beating had fallen on deaf ears, but outside the skilled, pitched slapping of fingers on hide and the deeper boom of the middle bass had served its purpose. Those awaiting the operation were kept completely separate from those who had already endured it. There was no need to unnecessarily frighten an already anxious mass. The older of the male slaves, although more resilient to pain, had by far the most painful experience to endure—perhaps this was fortuitous, Allah be praised—for they bled a lot, making it necessary to cauterize the wounds to obviate any infection.

Once the circumcisions had been performed it was then a matter of selecting those who would be suitable to become eunuchs.

This was a far more serious operation, as the male had to be castrated so that he would never again desire a woman, thereby causing no embarrassment in a household of many concubines. It was also believed that this desire was replaced with a great aptitude for strength, thus children on whom this operation was performed would grow to possess incomparable strength.

The severity of the operation often proved fatal, thus a fully recovered eunuch always fetched a high price on the markets of Dar es Salaam and Zanzibar.

This complete, a ceremony was held for those who had embraced Mohammed and were now true to the religion of Islam. Prayers were said, followed by showers of scents and spices on each and every person who had opened their hearts and minds to this world. Much feasting was held and although they would always be slaves, they would be entitled to the rights that were accorded to the believers of Islam.

VII

It was time to begin the next and final stage of this particular expedition. I had to get all the items of sale—slaves, ivory et cetera—to the coast at Dar es Salaam where Arab traders from Zanzibar and Arabia would be eagerly waiting to purchase these goods.

This took an inordinate amount of preparation. Each chief, whose land had to be traversed, required large sums of money or goods to allow us peaceful passage through his country. The levy depended on the size of the safari and for this reason all sick slaves, as well as those who were not likely to make the trip, were weeded out, as they would be costly on the journey and valueless on the market.

These unfortunates were taken by *askaris* to a place near the present *boma* of Tabora, known to the locals as the 'Hill of Death'. Here their legs were broken, preventing any mobility and thus any chance of escape. They were left to die in the dust like animals—no food, no water—facing a continual onslaught from the scavengers of Africa. It wouldn't take long for them all to be killed off, their flesh torn like carrion from their bodies by hideous Marabou storks; limbs bitten clean through by the powerful jaws of the hyenas, which, unthreatened by larger predators, would make short work of the numerous crippled forms. And all the while aided by their equally opportunistic counterparts, the jackals and the vultures.

Of the party I had brought back with me, some thirty-five were taken away to face this dreadful fate.

Because of such practices there were many animals that devoured human flesh—they had no fear of humans and gorged themselves on the writhing mass of humanity we left for them.

Some, facing the same fate, were fortunate to be purchased by local residents at very low prices. They would be hired out to passing travellers for the duration of their stay in Tabora. Should they prove unsatisfactory, they would be severely dealt with, even killed—though even this was preferable to being taken to the Hill of Death.

It would take us three months to get to the coast, three months of continuous walking. For the slaves, they suffered the additional burden of being tethered together like bovines, carrying weighty loads of ivory and other goods needed for trade en route.

We encountered our first difficulties near Dodoma. The chief of the tribe we were to rely on for hospitality mistakenly assumed that my competence as a negotiator matched my immaturity in years and demanded an outrageous amount of passage money. Many long hours were spent in the heat, both of us surrounded by a handful of fanning slaves and a few of our best *askaris*. The bargaining was fierce and taxing, but he had underestimated me and had to concede that I had the business acumen of a grown man.

And so it was for the next two-and-a-half-months that days

melted into one another, villages left behind blurring into one. The farther we walked the farther seemed our destination. It was only when our bargaining supplies dwindled that we realized how close to the coast we actually were. Slowly, almost imperceptibly, the vegetation changed—from open savannah grasslands to the dry acacia scrub of the baobab country—and now, with the occasional palm tree flanking us, our spirits lifted.

A day or so later, our path lined with lush palms, we knew it to be only a couple more days before we stood on the soft sands of the Indian Ocean.

The jubilant crack of gunfire whipped through the opaque coastal humidity as, finally, on the horizon we caught our first glimpse of the sea. Within a few hours we stood on the beach. The sand baked beneath our weary feet as we let the water lap against our legs, the realization that our journey had at last come to an end, sinking in. For most of us it was our first time at the sea, and a wondrous sight it was too—its vastness and striated hues almost impossible to fathom. As if from some faraway, hidden river, white crests of water incessantly rolled forward, one after another after another, and, at our feet stopping abruptly and retreating.

It was a still, hot day, with the moist, sticky air clinging to our bodies. How strange it was that heat should feel so different here from that in Tabora. Looking around me at my men I saw many were entertaining the very same thoughts, struck by the same wonder.

My father had given me a letter of introduction to Rashidi bin Hasim, an important and highly thought-of man in the area. Most notably, he knew all the buyers. For a small consideration he would help me obtain the best prices for my slaves and ivory. We arrived at his enclosure tired, footsore and welcoming a much-needed rest.

The slaves were divided up according to age and sex and locked in separate *bomas*. They were not allowed to communicate with one another. Many had sustained sores along the way where their harnesses had chaffed into their necks, rubbing the skin clean off. All such injuries, no matter how minor, had to be attended to so that when they stood on the platform for sale they would be in perfect condition with no disfigurement to lower their value. Apart from these wounds, some had developed serious cases of malaria and sleeping sickness. Victims of the latter, we knew, would not live. There was no cure for this terrible disease. Those who fell victim to it would become progressively thinner, wasting away to an inevitable death. Many *ngangas* had professed over the years to have found a cure, ghastly concoctions that proved to be of no avail.

The money spent on these slaves would, however, not be allowed to go to waste—through hiring them out to work parties a small portion of this could be recovered. They would be made to work until they could no longer swing a hoe or bend to weed crops without collapsing to the ground. Only then would they be banished to a separate enclosure for the incurables and permitted to die.

It was of the utmost importance at all times to remember that they were slaves, classified as little more than animals.

It was during my time in Dar es Salaam that I heard talk of the many white people making their homes in Zanzibar. I had heard talk of white people only once before, from my father. He had known of three white men and had in fact seen two of them.

One had accompanied a two-thousand-strong force of Arabs that was launching an attack on Chief Mirambo. After a three-month delay, as a result of the battle, this white man had gone on to Ujiji to search for another white man who was a great doctor and was said to be lost. The third had travelled through the Buha country. He was rumoured to be looking for a very big river that lay far away to the north. This was an area we rarely visited because the Waganda were a dangerous people with a wicked king.

The battle with Chief Mirambo came about as a result of the Arabs placing a puppet king on the throne at Tabora—a king who would permit them the freedom of travel and trade they believed they deserved. The former king, Fundi Kira, had been deposed because of the high taxes he had imposed on foreign goods passing through his territory. Fundi Kira, however, was not that easily dispatched and began launching covert attacks on itinerant Arab caravans and pursuant troops. This unrest allowed for the emergence of King Mirambo. Although a Wanyamwezi of noble birth, Mirambo had grown up among the Ngoni refugees from the south and had adopted their fiercely effective military tactics. Over a period of ten years he had conquered tribe after tribe, building for himself a vast empire. This power enabled him to exact exorbitant taxes from passing safaris, especially in the form of guns and gunpowder. Mirambo was proving to be the fly in the Arab trading ointment and hence the Arab attack, to which this first white man had attached himself.

The Dar es Salaam market was a seething mass of people and

flies, the latter far outnumbering the former. The market itself stretched across a massive area and presumably had grown to such an extent that it now, by default, incorporated all conceivable trading zones.

The first hint that one was nearing the market was the lingering, pungent odour that clung to the moisture in the air and intensified as one drew closer. At its foundation was the fetid smell of decaying vegetable matter and fish, caught fresh that morning but turned by heat and handling. The heat and humidity did nothing to preserve body odour and the putrid stench of fear from the slave quarters hung as an unnecessary pall around us. One would have expected the gentle sea breeze to mask the smells of the market to a certain degree, but all it did was cloak the odours in the sickly sweet scent of frangipani.

In an effort to attract more customers to one's stall it became necessary to shout to make oneself heard above the throng. Prices, special prices, unbelievable deals, dazzling, creative characteristics attached to goods one would find "nowhere else in Africa" were repeatedly called with blinding monotony. And above all this was the bellow of the auctions—slave and ivory alike. However unfavourable the market itself the atmosphere among the merchants and buyers was infectious.

It took some three weeks to sell all the slaves at a fine profit.

Arrangements were made for the return journey to Tabora. We had acquired so much at the market that we needed to hire additional porters to transport everything. These goods would be used for trading purposes and passage fees on the return journey, as well as to replenish supplies in Tabora.

The caravan on the day we started back was enormous. We were also accompanied by a fair number of hangers-on. These people wished to journey into the hinterland but were too afraid to do so alone. They had heard terrible stories in Dar es Salaam about the fearsome tribes living deep in the hinterland who, it was believed, mutilated the bodies of people they found along the route. There were stories about unfortunate travellers being dismembered by *ngangas* for rituals and medicines.

I had in my care many letters for people living in Tabora. I belonged to a family well known for its honesty and I could therefore be trusted to deliver them. Fifteen miles later we stopped at the village of the Jumbe. The headman was given a letter from the agent in Dar es Salaam and as a result knew better than to cause me any trouble. The many days that a safari takes to traverse the long miles between Dar es Salaam and Tabora passed slowly. Again the Wagogo demanded a hefty passage fee but I had made allowance for this.

One night, about three weeks' safari out of Tabora, lions raided our camp. Two porters and a night guard were dragged screaming into the night from under their blankets. Fires were lit and shots were fired into the blackness of the night but no sign of them was ever found. Occasionally an awful scream in the distance would cut through the night and further shots would be fired in the general direction.

After one such incident the unmistakable roar of a wounded lion fused with the cries of its prey. The following morning we ventured out to investigate. The remains of two victims were found—only shards of bone and bloodied bits of savaged hands and feet. The third body was found, almost untouched. A trail of blood led from the corpse into the bush, proving that our shots had wounded the beast.

We buried the remains of the victims near the road and built small stone cairns over the graves to indicate that they had died while on safari.

On nearing Tabora I sent two men ahead to inform my father of our coming. We were received in the usual jubilant manner— gunfire announcing our arrival and singing beckoning us nearer.

My father was well pleased with my work. I had shown a handsome profit.

There was much feasting that night and many tales recounted of the journey. I related the up-to-date news that I had received while at the port. In particular, much interest was shown when I told my father and other relatives about the white people who were settling in Zanzibar and befriending the Sultan. It was said that they were English and had many warships anchored at sea between the coast and the island, stopping dhows transporting slaves—and worse—freeing the slaves.

There was much alarm—this practice would bring ruin to many of us.

There was also talk of other white people, said to be German, who were showing much interest in the lands of Tanganyika. Their reputation did not paint a very comforting picture. Time after time I had been told how they were not like the English, that they were cruel, their discipline harsh and that they treated all with contempt and brutality.

PART II

VIII

I returned from one of my many safaris to find Tabora abound
with talk of white people making their way to our district. I
was told there had been fierce fighting with the Wagogo who
had suffered great defeat at the hands of these intruders. It was
said that the white people were moving at great speed towards
Unyanyembe with guns and equipment so powerful they could
knock down the biggest of houses, even those made of stone. They
had machines that could be heard from miles away and needed
only water and what they called petrol, to work. Altogether it
was very frightening. This disturbing news was brought to us by
safaris returning from the coast and from white deserters. As a
result we were all forbidden to go on safari to buy slaves and ivory.
It was thought best for all concerned. We should wait until the end
result was made clear to us. So for several months my brothers
and I and the rest of the family idly passed the time around the
town of Unyanyembe.

One day, late in the afternoon, a soft droning was carried into
the village on a late summer breeze. Some of the men walked to
the outskirts of the village and realized the droning was coming
from a long cloud of dust on the horizon. After standing watching
for a short while it was observed that the cloud was moving

significantly closer. The droning grew louder and turned itself into a most uncommon noise the closer the dust came. We didn't have to wait long before we saw our first caravan of white people and their machines.

We were curious—they had many things that no one in the village had seen before. We were keen to take a closer look but uncertainty and fear held us back. What were they doing here and more importantly what did they want from us? Little did we know that the town's name would be changed to that of Chief Tabora's, the Tabora I speak of today, and that it would become an important stronghold in supporting the German advance through our country.

They made themselves comfortable under tents of canvas near where the white doctor's, Livingstone's, *tembe* stood. This house had belonged to an Arab, a notorious slave-trader. Constructed of red clay, the house was built around a central courtyard beneath tall, shady mango trees. This was the only watering point for many miles and thus was the attraction for this curious caravan. We were informed that they were an advance guard for a caravan many times bigger that was travelling by foot with many porters. They instructed us to collect as much grain as possible as well as goats and chickens. We were paid for our produce with lengths of calico and other tradable items.

The dissipating heat did nothing to relieve our disquiet, as the sun slowly lowered itself over the horizon on the far side of town. The gusty winds were unsettling and made us nervous. The people of the village spoke in hushed tones over their cooking fires, men speculated among each other over the future and mothers kept their children close.

Not long after the advance guard had arrived, stirring up not only the dust but also the imaginations of the villagers, did the rest of the soldiers in the promised column materialize on the horizon. They wasted no time. We were all rounded up and told that we now belonged to the new government, the German government, and that we would all have to work for the invaders. No one in the community was spared this information—not the families of high standing, not the nobility, not the slaves, no one. We were all treated as one. This was frightening news, as we did not understand what it might entail. To those of us who had enjoyed the freedom and masterdom of the entire country of Unyamwezi this came as a shock. We were horrified that we now owed our allegiance to a so-called superior people.

Not then, as I was too consumed with the arrogance that accompanies status and wealth, but years later it struck me that, on that day when we were rounded up, we probably felt much the same as so many of the slaves who had been wrenched from their homes and families.

The Arabs did all they could to resist white rule. They refused to relinquish their right to claim taxes from passing caravans. One sizeable uprising was led by a prominent sugar-plantation owner. Agents working for the German East Africa Company were killed or driven away, the mission at Dar es Salaam was attacked and priests killed. But ultimately the Arab warlord was forced to surrender to the superior German forces and summarily executed. Contributing to his defeat was the fact that many Germans had befriended local girls, thereby diluting local allegiances.

It was after this that we learned of the harshness of the German conquerors. Arab shops were closed down and their goods confiscated. They were forced to work as labourers, like the rest of us.

The next ten years were to be some of the most trying times we had ever experienced. The German governor did not display many savoury or sympathetic characteristics. He boasted openly how he enjoyed killing Africans. In addition, the land was engulfed by a series of natural disasters. Most of the cattle were slain by an indiscriminate illness, known as rinderpest by the white people. Men, women and children were cut down by a vicious smallpox epidemic and our crops levelled by plagues of locusts. Year after year the rains stayed away, bringing no relief to the ever-increasing number of diseases, or to the people left starving in the villages. Many previously inhabited areas reverted to bush. But this only compounded the problems—for the tsetse fly then moved in.

The first major task we were forced to undertake was to cut the forest lines on top of the hill that overlooked the flatlands surrounding the village of Unyanyembe. It was on this hill that we were to build Fort Tabora. It took many, many weeks of slaving in the unrelenting sun, hour after hour. Any man caught resting or slackening his pace was severely beaten.

During this time the Germans brought in, by wagons, porters, mules and donkeys, many tons of cement, food, arms and ammunition. We absorbed all this with mixed emotion—we were intrigued and I must admit, at times, impressed by what we saw—the building techniques and the variety of arms. Up to that point we had only been exposed to muzzle-loaders. The Germans were by turns kind and cruel. Those who did not follow their instructions or defied them were either beaten or sent to what they called 'gaol'. With the cement that was brought in and with rocks that were carved from the hillside, laboriously hewn with hammers and chisels, we built the big fort of Tabora.

The fort was about two hundred yards long in one direction and one hundred and fifty yards in the other. It was in the shape of a long box. The walls were about a yard thick and spaced around them were special towers where sentries stood guard. As a result of the positioning of these towers the Germans were able to view the entire countryside, in a full circle, around the fort. In this way they would be forewarned should any hostile army advance on the town.

Inside the fort there were sleeping places for the men, dining rooms, kitchens, and special strong rooms where they kept their arms and ammunition. There were also the rooms they used as gaols. Near the parapets, which were seventeen feet high, were special walkways on the inside for the sentries to patrol.

When the Germans called for volunteers to become soldiers I felt I was already used to such a life and enlisted for two reasons— firstly, I was ready for a change and secondly, I believed greater freedoms would come of this new position. I was readily accepted by the Germans and was thus inducted into their ranks.

Training lasted many months. We were taught how to march properly, how to handle a variety of weapons and most importantly, how to be fearless. The training was so intense that at times when I fell down to sleep I often wondered whether I'd made a wise choice. Our instructors were ruthless and cruel. It seemed they did not know how to speak. It intrigued me that it was necessary for all orders to be shouted. The smallest mistake was punished with hard labour, not only for the culprit but for all of us.

No part of our training ever took place in the shade. At weapons' instruction one day, with the sun bearing down, we were being taught how to strip and assemble a Mauser rifle. That particular day was indescribably hot, and sweat poured from us as we knelt in the dust at the mercy of the sun. Perspiration ran down our foreheads, stinging our eyes. The heat and not a little bit of nervousness made our hands so clammy that we handled our rifles like a father holding his newborn child for the first time. They slipped from our grasp, clattering to the ground as we desperately tried to wipe dry our hands on our sweat-soaked clothing. The instructor's screaming was deafening, nearing hysteria, spit flying from his mouth as he ranted. This was early in our training and we did not understand why he was so angry when the problem seemed quite clear. But none of us was about to open his mouth and tell this frantic, sunburned white man that it was simply too hot.

During this time, travellers who had journeyed up from the coast told of big steam-and-iron horses that ran on steel rails—that were being off-loaded at the docks. Other big news was that a road was being constructed between Dar es Salaam and Morogoro.

One day, a number of us were chosen by the Germans to guard a big safari that consisted of white soldiers and other men whose job it was to look through strange glasses that allowed one to see farther than normally possible. After studying the land through these glasses the men had to 'draw' lines through the bush. There were to be two parties—one to move east from Tabora and the other, to which I was assigned, west towards Ujiji.

We were woken by the sound of the reveille bugle. We fell into line, carrying with us our blankets and eating utensils. Our instructions were to march to a certain village where we would be met by a number of hired porters. They would be carrying food, guns and the instruments necessary to complete our mission. We moved towards Usenge, a village some one hundred miles from Tabora and well known to me from my slave-raiding days. The going was not too difficult as the path was a well-worn slave-route and we arrived at Usenge after just six days.

Our arrival was met with mixed feeling. Chief Msenge was visibly perturbed at seeing such a large, well-armed and well-disciplined force accompanied by so many porters and men, for whom he would be called upon to supply hefty quantities of food. It was obvious by the puffed-out chests, simmering eyes and arms at the ready that some of his men had wanted to put up a fight. The Germans were impatient with such behaviour and allowed them little time to entertain hostile thought. They made it quite clear that they meant business and were not there for the welfare of Chief Msenge. There was work to be done and they were determined to see that the great path that lay ahead was completed as a matter of priority.

From Usenge we moved on to Malagaraise, some three days' march in distance. Some of the white men were now starting to suffer from the heat, mosquitoes and tsetse fly. They had angry, open sores over their bodies where the flies would congregate.

They must have been in a great deal of discomfort but these strange white men were dogmatic in their approach and were able to steel themselves against personal pain. We Africans were used to such hardships, borne under this unforgiving sun. I must admit that my respect for these men grew in some measure as the days passed. They were strong and possessed a courage I had seldom seen. There was no question of discipline slackening or taking shorter marches. Those who could no longer walk, whether on account of sores or disease, were carried on *mashilas*. At each village we came to additional porters were sought to perform these extra functions.

When we arrived at Malagaraise, a village close to the swamplands surrounding the Malagaraise River, no time was wasted in preparing to cross. Rafts were made from the branches of felled trees tied together with thongs of animal hide.

The heat clung to one's body in the swamp as a pungent odour clings to a bloated elephant two days dead. The weeds, the reeds, the thick vegetation were so closely entwined, seemingly to deliberately deny our passage. Patches of swamp were doused in a blinding stench, perhaps rotting vegetation, perhaps a crocodile's prey, a carcass carefully stowed away to slowly rot. The going was so arduous that often men would have to get off and wade waist-deep in mud and water, pushing the rafts from the rear and clearing a reasonable path in the front. In silence we each considered the various dangers this task bore. There was no telling how deep the water was at any one point, a few feet of mud could easily engulf a man's head. The waters could be infested with indiscriminate crocodiles, or perhaps they preferred the clearer waters of the river farther on. All we had to go on were the stories we'd heard—and our fertile imaginations.

After one such difficult stretch the men got back on the raft and to their horror saw they were covered in leeches. Most froze momentarily, considering the best option to rid themselves of these bloodsuckers. One man, in a moment of panic, grabbed at a leech on his arm and ripped it off. His mistake immediately became apparent as in his hand he held the squirming body and in his arm the head remained. The acidic juice of a local plant had to be applied, forcing the leech to withdraw its head and only then could it be pulled off.

There was no stopping, no turning back and when we again reached a place where we had to get off the raft to free it from a web of weeds, we did so with more trepidation than before. Ahead of us some porters had had to disembark. We were quickly torn from our terrified reveries by an awful scream and a large splash in the deeper waters. We strained to see and then it came again, the splash with a glint of creamy white underbelly.

A crocodile had grabbed hold of a porter's leg and was going about the business of drowning him. Rolling over and over in the water, arms flailing, the porter stood no chance against the power of his killer. We stood frozen in horrified silence, knowing that at any moment any one of us might be next. The scene before us was so brutal, so grossly disparate. Then suddenly, both porter and crocodile disappeared, leaving behind a most unsettling silence. We later learned that crocodiles had eaten several of the porters during this part of the journey.

When we eventually reached dry land we were re-grouped into

columns and the march resumed, farther and farther towards
the west. We followed a route not far from the Malagaraise River
itself, as this was the easiest ground on which to walk. It was not
as heavily forested as the higher ground in the distance towards
the north.

Three days after crossing the river we came to the small Arab
settlement of Uvinza. This is where the Arabs produced salt from
a spring that bubbled out of a hillside a few hundred yards from
the river. Since this appeared to be an important place the officer
commanding the safari decided to call a rest and make this the
headquarters of the team, now called surveyors. We enjoyed a
welcome week of rest. The sick were attended to and our supplies
replenished. The white men climbed the surrounding hills
with their telescopes, apparently making many, very important
observations, which they then recreated on paper over many,
many hours.

When the commanding officer was satisfied that the sick had
been catered for and that the tribes surrounding the makeshift
headquarters were not hostile, he arranged for some three-
quarters of the safari to proceed to Ujiji. I had made this trip many
times, not always on quite the same path as we now followed
but I knew the land through which we were to travel. I knew
of the lion-infested forests—forests that had to be hacked at to
allow passage and forests in which roamed the marauding Buha
nomads. Crossing this country surpassed anything these white
men had ever experienced or indeed imagined. It was not simply
a question of heat and tsetse fly, although these factors were ever-
present, but of dreadful dangers to life and limb.

Two and a half weeks later we viewed from the hills of the Lake Tanganyika escarpment the little village of Ujiji. I learned that it was here that the two white men my father had spoken of, Doctor David Livingstone and Mr. Henry Morton Stanley, had first met.

On arrival some of us were instructed to go on ahead and instruct the villagers to produce food for the safari. Goats, chickens and even fish were to be supplied to feed the soldiers. The local Arabs tried to stop the villagers from obeying. It was necessary—since Ujiji was so remote—for the officer commanding the safari to make it perfectly clear to the locals, villagers and Arabs alike, who was in charge and that dissent would not be tolerated. The Arabs who tried to resist this sudden invasion of their land and dilution of their power were severely flogged.

These floggings always took place publicly.

IX

From Ujiji small bands of surveyors went out and scrutinized the countryside—the level of the ground and the direction in which lay the delta of the Malagaraise River. After this work was completed it was decided that the whole company would move to an area closer to the mouth of the river on the shores of Lake Tanganyika, between two ranges of hills that swept down to the water. It was here that we built the second fort, called Kigoma.

From Kigoma the safari moved in an easterly direction, spending days at a time in one place while the survey teams took levels and planned the route for the railway line that was to be built. Of course, many of the locals clearly thought every one of us had gone quite mad. They did not know what was in the white man's mind. What we were doing had not been explained to them and they had no concept of what would be derived from this pioneering work. We climbed hills, sometimes many miles from the actual direction that the railway line was to traverse. With a smaller band of surveyors, some of us *askaris* were detailed to go out and shoot game to feed the many porters and servants. Much of the country we explored had never been walked upon, not even by Africans—virgin land, untouched and savage. During this time white men and Africans were stricken with sleeping sickness.

After the third month, we knew we could not be too far from Uvinza. We reached a place where the valley, cut by the Malagaraise River, spread out to form a circular clearing, surrounded on all sides by hills, through which the river meandered.

My section received instructions to travel south and then strike east to rejoin the main team. Food was never a problem, for the game was plentiful and we killed what we needed.

However, on the four-day journey south we found no water. By the final day it was becoming difficult to swallow our own saliva, which was fast drying up as our bodies had become so dehydrated. We marched on, delirious with thirst, the bush around us taking on a surreal quality. Our attentions were constantly drawn to movements and shapes that on closer inspection proved elusive. We started not to believe our own eyes. The ceaseless plodding up and down mountains and the endless struggle against sickness and disease was compounded a hundred-fold by the lack of water. The dust was in our mouths, up our noses, clouding our eyes. Our eyes and noses stung and the tongue in my mouth was rough and thick. My lips were cracked through to the flesh where flies now congregated. Fatigue prohibited me from brushing them away. As one we stopped, the unmistakable gurgling of water was coming from a short way ahead. We ran and, when we saw the water, fell to our knees and drank hungrily. After drinking deeply, the realization hit home that the water tasted like oil. The officer in charge struck a match, threw it onto the surface and immediately a blaze flared up. The fire burning on top of the water was carried downstream and eventually died out.

You can well imagine the pangs of thirst we now felt. Half-crazed we began digging some ten paces from the spring. As the ground got muddier we dug more fervently. The water we found was drinkable and we drank till we felt sick.

We spent two days resting at this spot and then changed course, walking with the morning sun warming our faces. All the while the survey officer took readings on the sun from mountaintops, and on the stars when the sun had pulled closed its blanket. He told us he was able to tell exactly where we were on the earth's surface (not that this meant all that much to us at the time).

We came across elephant not far from an unknown village. But our attentions were soon diverted when we met tribesmen who had taken up arms and hidden their women and children. After extensive discussions between one of our porters who spoke the Buha language and one of their senior-ranking guards, it transpired they had never before seen or heard of white people. They feared we were a slave-raiding party. Our mission was explained to them but they still appeared suspicious. To extend a hand of friendship and avoid a bloody slaughter we offered to take them with us on an elephant hunt. It was clear from his tone and gesticulating that our translator was having to employ all his powers of persuasion to get the villagers to agree.

After some time two men stepped forward, either out of curiosity or bravado, and agreed to accompany us. It was clear that the elephants had been causing a lot of damage to the village crops. The thought of destroying these brutes, which were destroying their livelihood, appealed to them and at the same time they would be able to replenish their meat supplies. About a mile and a half from the village we found the herd moving quietly through the shade of some fever trees. The officer, with two other white men, crept up to the elephants and with their light rifles felled two with ease. They collapsed to the ground, dead and heavy, dust exploding around them. This surprised many of us, especially the accompanying villagers. We had always hunted with the more cumbersome muzzle-loaders. With bigger barrels and bigger bullets they were rarely able to kill an elephant with a single shot. The villagers were truly delighted.

They would not allow us to approach or cut up the carcasses, warning us of the dangers of the spirits that lived on in the fallen beasts, even after death. They insisted that these spirits had first to be disposed of by the village *nganga*.

The tusks were of a fair size and would certainly pay the masters well for their labour and efficiency in shooting the troublesome elephants. When the rest of the villagers arrived the usual rituals were observed and only then was the meat cut up and taken back to the village. We were instructed by our senior officer to make camp for the night.

Because of the necessity to dry meat while travelling in the bush, it was decided that we would stay on another day and a night to complete the task. Porters and *askaris* were sent into the bush to cut dry brushwood and stakes on which to skewer the meat. Great fires were built around the staked meat so that it would smoke and dry, preventing it from going bad.

On the morning of the third day we left this isolated village and headed towards Uvinza. At midday we arrived unexpectedly on the edge of an escarpment. The sky was clear and bright with low wisps of cloud hugging the surrounding mountains. The valley where the little village of Uvinza lay was brightly lit, as though Allah himself was taking a closer look. The land around the village was fertile and cultivated. The bush, in stark contrast to the orderly gardens, was a dishevelled brown–green mass that threatened to engulf all in its course, creeping across the valley floor and disappearing around the corners of the imposing mountains.

It appeared we had an easy day's walk ahead of us but, on descending the escarpment, we found ourselves entering dense, tall elephant grass and impenetrable thorn bush. The grass cut through our flesh. Even the heavy boots supplied by the German army could not stand up to this harsh terrain.

After battling this monster of nature for some eight hours we were still several miles from our crossing point on the Malagaraise River, its unfurling, pervasive swamps still ahead, a terrifying abomination. The memory of our previous crossing was still fresh and the closer we got the higher rose the bile in our throats.

We arrived at its banks at dusk. It was here that we should have met the main body of the expedition which had taken a more direct route from Kigoma. We fired our guns into the air to signal that we had at last arrived and to give an estimate on our position. To our consternation we heard no gunfire in return. No welcoming shots, just the ringing silence that followed our exclamation.

Were we too late? Had we missed them as a result? Perhaps we were too early?

The officer was worried, now facing a weighty decision. Should we move on to Uvinza in the hope that they had already crossed the river, having tired of waiting for us? Or did we wait? Our instructions were to meet the main body a day's march from Uvinza—our present position. Instructions were there to be obeyed. After careful deliberation it was decided we would wait for one passing of the moon and one of the sun.

Our night was troubled by hippos and lions. Sitting around the cooking fires that night we were glad of this fortuitous period of rest, although our minds were crowded with thoughts of what might be delaying the others. Staring into the fires, each man picturing in the flames that licked at the night air his own version of events, we were jolted back to reality by heavy grunting and bellowing coming from the riverbanks. Hippos are fearless and when it comes to the matter of their nightly feeding, there is nothing—besides a bullet, I suppose—that can stand in their way. For reasons that are too complex and perhaps as yet unresolved in my mind, I cannot fully explain why I always found charging hippos more frightening than charging elephants. Perhaps it is that elephants charge to protect and hippos to destroy.

When the charge came it was deafening, with the hippos paying no heed to the thick bush that separated them from their target—us. The agitated rustling of grass and shrubs indicated their advance. We were well trained for any split-second eventuality and assumed a defensive position, directly facing the oncoming charge. Rifles were fired into the air as well as toward the rapidly approaching beasts. But they would not be stopped—unless a bullet actually found its mark. They careened into the campsite and toward the cooking fires. Porters screamed, gunfire whipped and cracked all about as the hippos pounded the earth, seeking to destroy whatever came into their path. It was pandemonium. As we lost our grip on the situation so the panic rose. Porters fled in all directions, screaming hysterically, attracting fatal attention to themselves. The hippos stomped angrily on the cooking fires, burning themselves, incensing them further, and tearing through the camp with blinding aggression before disappearing into the blackness of the night.

We killed one hippo and they killed two porters. We doused the fires for the night to avoid a similar onslaught but were now vulnerable to lions. The darkness pressing in on our campsite hung thick with the smell of fresh blood, hippo and human. It was not only lions we attracted that night, but hyena and jackals too, in fact just about any night predator unable to resist the mantle of darkness and the sweet allure of recent slaughter. There were many of us who had spent many a night in the remotest of bush plagued by dangerous animals, but to the *wapagazii* this was not familiar, it was terrifying. But what were their choices? The place where they found themselves was so remote, so densely populated with wild animals, so incredibly hostile that to run and take their chances alone would surely be suicide.

We set off the next day following the southern bank of the river, forcing our way through reeds and undergrowth. The riverbank was alive with birds and animals. Late that evening we neared Uvinza. About a quarter of a mile outside the village we fired our guns, announcing our presence. And so it was that we had arrived at the midway stage of the survey of the railway line between Kigoma and Tabora.

The following day the searing midday sun highlighted a

dishevelled and virtually broken group of men making their way toward us. It was our officer and his retinue, but from the look of them it was obvious that their journey had been hard and unforgiving. Their numbers had dwindled considerably and of those who had made it back, many were stricken with the deadly sleeping sickness. There was nothing that could be done, it was the command of Allah and He, no doubt, would release their souls into His haven of peace.

We stayed at Uvinza for two weeks. Thereafter, it was time to return, the way we had originally travelled. There was no other route the railway line could take. On the way back the white men continually went out and ordered lines of trees to be chopped down, all the time taking endless readings through their telescopes. This took many days of hard and tedious work—in the hottest months of the year.

We arrived at the main depot in Tabora four months later. During this time the rains had started and we had buried many porters and *askaris* en route. Truly, they were to be future landmarks and a symbol of the courage, endurance and co-operation between the white men and the Africans who had participated in this grand adventure, a pioneering advancement in the development of Tanganyika.

As a result of the prevailing conditions of the heavy rains we were granted permission to take leave. We went home where we used the time fruitfully to dig our gardens, repair our houses and attend to other such chores.

The *askaris* who had died on the safari were mourned by their loved ones, who blamed their deaths on the white men, accusing them of savagery and cruelty. They could not reconcile their loss with the irreversible onslaught of European civilization.

This brings to an end the first stage of the railway line from Dar es Salaam to Kigoma.

X

When the rains dried up the commanding officer received a message from Dar es Salaam ordering him to attend a conference there. He was asked to bring with him as much of the survey material as possible. He selected a number of *askaris* to accompany him on the journey, of which I was one. An entire company was to stay behind in Tabora as a deterrent against a possible power struggle between the Arabs and the various warlike tribes that were still a presence.

We were called to attention on parade and instructed to recruit porters from the surrounding villages. This took only a couple of days as most of us had been avidly involved in slave-raiding and were known to most of the local villagers. There was no problem recruiting five hundred porters.

There was one village though that would not roll over, Ihonda. In bygone days I was accustomed to entering a village and taking it by force through the sheer superiority of my force. This time was different as there were only three *askaris* under my command, however, this time we were armed with the latest German rifles—Mausers.

Some women and children tending crops spotted our approach. They ran screaming back to the settlement, warning others of our coming. We were still a way off and the tribesmen had plenty of time to gather their bows and arrows and present a formidable defence. All we had going for us was that they had no idea how many of us there were. They had seen our uniforms and assumed we were some kind of united, formal raiding party. We crouched low in the scrub and observed the villagers for a while—assessing how many porters we could glean from the village, how many armed men there were and where the headman was. Women were running wildly, screaming for their children who were also running in panic, screaming for their mothers. Panic in the village would work to our advantage. We estimated there were about two hundred men with bows and arrows. As had been drilled into me by our instructors, we spread out—two men to my left and one to my right. If we were to fire upon the village it was important for them to think they were surrounded, so we spread out as far as possible without losing touch. We advanced slowly, keeping our bodies pressed close to the earth, using the available bush as camouflage. About fifty paces out of the village I gave the order to stop.

All was quiet as hundreds of pairs of eyes tried in vain to penetrate the dense bush and identify anything out of place—a shadow, a silhouette, the stray reflection of the sun off a metallic surface.

From my position I called for the headman to order his men to throw down their weapons. I explained our superior weaponry to him, emphasizing the power and ability to shoot through barricades. But he just laughed. He said that if we wanted slaves we would have to take them from over the dead bodies of his villagers. I took my time. We were few and could not surround the village but we needed to convince this defiant headman of our strength. I inhaled deeply, unblinking. Imperceptibly I turned to my left and then to my right. These were good men. It was inevitable that we would have to open fire on these people or be killed ourselves.

In silence we moved forward, taking cover as we advanced, all the while narrowing the distance between the villagers and us. Unfortunately, one of the men to my left was spotted and a loud cry went up, followed by a shower of arrows. Fortunately none found its mark. Our position had been compromised and we were still too far away to show any kind of strength. There was no question about it—we had to get closer. The villagers were now taking aim and arrows came whistling through the air, impaling the trees and earth around us. I slouched low behind a fallen branch and realized I had barely breathed since deciding to advance further. I exhaled slowly, reassessing our position. We were now within easy reach of the bowmen and I shouted to my comrades to fire four rounds of ammunition into the mass assembled in front of us.

The effect was instantaneous and brutal as the bullets ripped through the front line of villagers, some still poised with bow and arrow in hand. Some ten men fell. Some died on impact and others lay writhing in the dust, death standing over them— eclipsing the sun.

Arrows and spears rained down on us, sprung from the bow of contempt and fist of anger.

I instructed the two *askaris* on either flank to encircle the village and shout loudly in the process in order to create the illusion that we were a formidable force of at least a score of men.

Astoundingly, this ruse had its desired effect and the headman came forward, holding his spear above his head. This indicated he was willing to capitulate. I again told him to order his men to throw down their weapons a few feet ahead of their front line of defence.

This man was no stranger to me and I had full and clear recollection of his slyness from the days when I commanded great safaris. He begged for mercy, pleading for the lives of his villagers. How was he to protect his people if his guards were unarmed? Over the years he had become transparent to me and, had he known to whom he was talking, perhaps he would have admitted defeat sooner. From my concealed position I stood my ground, unbending. I told him he was now within range and the target of many riflemen. He was to command his men as I had bidden or face the wrath of our guns.

He did as he was told. We watched carefully until all the arms were heaped on the ground. Only then did I shout to my men to gather on me and move in on the assembled villagers.

Their terror turned to amazement when they saw there were only four of us, finding it difficult to comprehend the extraordinary fire-power of our rifles. I explained to the headman the purpose of our mission. At first he scoffed, refusing to co-operate, the arrogance I had known so well growing out of his initial fear.

"How can so many of us be subjugated by so few?" he asked his people theatrically. "What is this *askari* slave-trader talking about? White people who have come and conquered us and in their strength have demanded that we enslave ourselves without first having negotiated a purchase price?"

Simultaneously I levelled my gaze with his, my rifle trained on his chest. Like grass parting the crowd behind him moved back and out of the way. They were all vulnerable and, whether they moved aside or not, they had thrown down their weapons and so were rendered powerless. I instructed my men to tie up the headman and told him he would be the first of the new recruits to carry the belongings of the new white masters.

One by one the villagers came forward, offering their services. We assembled as many as were required, told them to collect their belongings from their huts and return to where we were holding the headman hostage. Once assembled, we set off to join the main force waiting for us at Tabora.

We arrived without incident and the commanding officer signed the new porters on at a wage equal to five shillings per month. They were also issued with blankets and uniforms. We then received our orders. We were to leave for Dar es Salaam in two days' time. All equipment and belongings were to be measured out so that no porter carried more than twenty kilograms.

The following day the camp was alive with activity. Men strode around this way and that, purposefully going about their business. Others milled about trying to look busy, but in some cases were not too sure what they should be doing. Orders were given, instructions obeyed. Rations for the first week were issued by the quartermaster, ammunition was checked, guns cleaned ... we eventually reached the stage when we no longer knew what still had to be done, what had been attended to and what we thought had been attended to but had in fact not.

The third day rose hot and early. Out of the previous two days' chaos, order was born and the long march to Dar es Salaam got underway.

From a distance the retinue must have looked like a giant millipede, surging left then right in a hypnotic sway.

Water on a safari with five or six hundred people was at a premium so for that reason we were only able to move in stages. Naturally, after the first three hours the porters' muscles started to burn and a halt had to be called so that the loads could be redistributed. Because of the type of country that lay ahead and the dangers that we were liable to encounter, the officer ordered a lieutenant, twenty porters and six *askaris* to proceed ahead, blazing a trail and forewarning any villagers en route of the necessity for a good supply of grain and water to be made available.

Because of my knowledge of the route, having made the trip to Dar es Salaam many times in the past, I was appointed head scout. After a short break twenty-seven scouts, a lieutenant and I moved off. The rains over the past few months had left the bush a self-contained, impenetrable jungle. It was always when passing through terrain like this that we were never certain of the dangers we might encounter.

I was assigned two *askaris*, a kind of advance party to the advance party. One *askari* was to walk some ten paces ahead of me and the other a few yards behind. We were moving through dry scrub, our army-issue boots crunching the stubble on the side of the path. The first intimation of danger was the distant, directionless collision of some unknown bulk against bark, followed immediately by the dry snapping of branches and the thunderous rush of feet or hooves through the grass. I was still trying to ascertain where the noise was coming from when an unmistakable snorting raised alarm bells in my head. No sooner had I established what was coming headlong towards us than the leading *askari* dashed past me, arms flailing. The dread set in, not knowing the direction of the charge. I must have cocked my rifle quickly but at the time my fingers felt numb and lazy. I was ready though, instinct overshadowing panic, steadying my hand and clearing my head. When the rhino did break through its grassy cover, head down in a blind rage, I was facing more or less the right direction and fired on impulse. No sooner had I pulled the trigger than I too rushed to get out of its way, screaming warnings to those behind me. No doubt my shout and the terrified screams of my *askari* had alerted the lieutenant to the danger thundering down on them. My round had found its mark, of that I had no doubt. It had been too close to miss. But a single shot did not have the power to bring down an animal of that size. Hopefully, the wound had slowed its pace and perhaps even set it off course. This would give us the chance to kill it without any loss of life on our side. Most of the porters had vanished, scattered to various perceived places of safety. The lieutenant, an excellent and experienced rifleman, fired two rapid shots at the animal, the first ripping into its leg, causing it to stumble and the next killed it. Aside from the rhino having impaled one of the porter's loads on its horn during its stampede, no serious injury or damage had been sustained.

Our progress was now halted in order to remove the valuable rhino horn and cut meat for the evening's meal. Although this took some hours, we were still some way ahead of the others. This was not the concern; the fact that we were still quite some distance from the next water point was. There was no question we had to reach water, even if it meant breaking the most revered rule of Africa—not travelling at night. Her dangers were challenging enough by day but at night the odds were all in her favour.

The porters were now carrying more than their allocated share but there was no griping, no moaning. They would have a good meal that night.

From our rear, dusk crept slowly upon us, our shadows lengthening perceptibly, the glare softening, turning the light first amber then rose and eventually a deepening blush. The sun had already fallen and the greying night-light consumed the day. We had still not reached water or a village. The lieutenant took the lead and guided the party by compass.

The fading gloom was alive with the night. Lions roared close by and every now and then the crashing of wild animals could be heard as they stampeded off into the bush—having picked up our scent and our noise. It was never certain which way these animals were running and because of the imaginary dangers taking seed in our minds the whole party closed ranks into very tight formation. As a result we kept tripping over each other's feet.

We marched like this until the lieutenant ordered a halt and summoned me. He asked me if I could smell burning wood. I lifted my head to the cool night air and, sure enough, the distinct smell of smoke from cooking fires filled my nostrils. This presented a further source of worry. We did not know whether we were approaching a village or if the smoke was coming from the camp of a hunting party or a raiding party preparing an attack on a nearby village. Another man and I were told to move closer, exercising care and caution, in order to establish what lay ahead. We removed our boots as well as excess clothes so that we could move forward noiselessly, but kept our bandoliers of ammunition. Quietly, with our bodies blending with the darkness we set off, rifles in one hand and the lieutenant's torch in the other. We were to walk a hundred paces at a time and, if all was clear, flash the torch back to the lieutenant, indicating that the rest of the men could advance too.

In this manner we were able to cover some eight hundred paces. Gardens of maize and millet and kasava indicated that a village lay ahead, invisible in the dark. The problem now was how to approach the village without raising the alarm and possibly inviting a mass attack against us. The tribespeople in this area were not completely ignorant of the German presence so the lieutenant decided that three of us would move forward in silence and approach the few men who were sitting around the dying embers of a fire in front of one of the huts.

Since we no longer showed up white in the darkness and our boots no longer gave us away we went unnoticed. We first circumvented the village, noting various small fires and their positions. Around two of these fires we noticed a few villagers squatting. It was late and we could not delay too long. We had already seen a man stand, stretch and yawn and head off into the bush to relieve himself before retiring to his hut.

We slipped closer, taking cover behind the nearest hut. Moving quickly, we arrested the man who had stepped into the perimeter of the bush. Strong hands suppressed his struggling and any calls of distress were muffled by a hand clapped across his mouth. Holding him down we informed him that we had firearms and that if he did not follow our instructions to the letter we would torch the village. He realized at once that we were serious and clearly did not want to be responsible for the deaths of so many men, women and children. He nodded furtively in agreement.

He was to go to the hut where his friends were squatting, call one of them over from the fireside and tell him that he had heard a distressing sound in the bush but could not place it. I warned him that I would be around the side of the hut and would be able to hear every hushed word spoken—a precaution in case he decided to disobey me and incite an attack. His friend was then to call the others and they were to head over to a designated tree on the outskirts, some ten paces from the nearest hut. There he was to explain to them that some people had arrived in the dark but that they meant no harm unless they, the villagers, wanted to fight. The strangers had come in peace and had no intention of ravaging the village of its food, women and children. While this was taking place we took up strategic positions so that we could monitor the situation. Any false move and we would open fire.

As the five men stood huddled under the tree I showed myself and introduced myself to them. As one their initial reaction was fear and flight, the former we would try to allay but to the latter would be shown no mercy. I wanted to be taken to the headman's hut. But none spoke or made any indication that they were ready to co-operate with me. After a little persuasion one man stepped forward and quietly led the way, the cold steel of my bayonet digging into the flesh between his shoulder blades, hard enough to remind him that there were to be no sudden acts of bravery or defiance. Once at the hut he would call out to the headman. All the while my *askaris* would have me covered with their rifles.

The man's four friends stayed behind as hostages, and any deviation in the plan would result in their immediate deaths.

On knocking on the door a couple of times an elderly man appeared, spear in hand. I had remained hidden from view and the old man did not suspect any danger. It was only after he had moved a few paces out of the doorway that I stepped forward, introduced myself and told him of our intentions.

I watched the slow transition from sleep to suspicion to defiance in his eyes and wasted no time in explaining to him his predicament.

Once the reasons for our night visit were clear I led him and the other man back to the group of waiting villagers and *askaris*. We all then, under close guard, proceeded to where the lieutenant lay in wait. My report contained little detail. No alarm had been raised; we had the headman hostage and needed therefore to expect no trouble.

A small conference was held with the headman in the presence of the other five men. Our mission was explained and our meagre requests agreed to. The headman also agreed to still any fears the villagers might entertain on seeing such a safari.

Thus we entered the village and he remained true to his word. The five men were told to wake a few people to produce water for us and some families were moved elsewhere to find shelter for the night, giving us a few huts in which to rest.

We settled down to a good meal and a full night's rest.

XI

Our departure the following morning was slightly delayed as the lieutenant detailed a few of the *askaris* to take the villagers back to the site where we had killed the rhino. We said our goodbyes at about midday.

The ensuing days passed in much the same manner until some weeks later we arrived in the flat country around Dodoma where water was scarce and game plentiful. Venison became our trading commodity for water. The area was scarred by the mark of the old slave traders. Many of the people had themselves been slaves. They were of mixed blood, their attitudes meek and it was seldom that these locals refused any of our requests or demands.

The going was hard through this country, the sun was remorseless and water points a great distance from one another. We fulfilled our orders and forewarned each village of the approach of the rest of the party, ensuring that they would prepare and have ample supplies of food and water available. Four days of this hard, heavy going brought us to kinder country, however, populated with the cruel and unforgiving Wagogo, the most warlike tribe between Kigoma and Dar es Salaam. The Wagogo had not accepted the authority of the Germans and it was entirely likely that we would meet warring parties.

In more hilly country we camped by a spring. As usual the lieutenant detailed sentries for the night's watch. We had settled down for our night's rest and, apart from the roaring of a lion, a nearby hyena chuckling at the hilarity of it all, and the noises of various night birds, there was no indication that any unpleasant incident was about to befall us. The campfire was burning itself down and the sentry, who could be seen with his rifle sloped, his shadow occasionally thrown up by a sporadic burst of flame from the fire, moved up and down on his beat. In this apparently peaceful atmosphere all but the sentry fell asleep. But it was not to last. Sometime during the hours before the first rooster crow the darkness fell too silent.

A shout from the sentry woke a few of us, but since it was not repeated we weren't sure whether we had dreamed it or whether it was real—that the sentry had been warning us of intruders. After a moment's careful consideration I decided, knowing how dangerous this country was, that it would be better to get up and investigate. Softly I called out to the sentry a number of times and was met by an unnerving silence. I knew something had to be drastically wrong but was unsure whether he had been silenced by man or beast.

Taking care not to show myself in the flickering flames of the dying fire, I took my rifle and bandolier and woke the lieutenant and the other members of the party. He and the *askaris* took up rifles and bandoliers, keeping low, with the lieutenant in front as we skirted the perimeter of the camp. We dared not make a sound, not even to call the missing sentry. The lieutenant halted and we listened for a few minutes. To our right we heard a faint noise caused by the disturbance of dried leaves and grass. The canopy of trees and thick bush shielded us from the scant light provided by the waning moon and it was difficult to tell what had made the sound. There had been signs of lion earlier and had they still been around they would have picked up our scent and moved off, even if it meant leaving their prey. On the other hand it could have been the careless footfall of a member of a Wagogo raiding party. The only way to tell would be to compromise our position and use the lieutenant's torch, a decision that now befell the lieutenant. In a barely audible whisper he asked me what I made of the noise.

I was intimately knowledgeable about the African bush and my instinct said human. Had it been a lion it would have moved again, or growled, but this had not happened. The sound had come only once. This left us with a score of new uncertainties of the potential enemy—their numbers, their exact whereabouts, the fate of the sentry and his rifle and whether he was dead or had been taken captive. I explained to the lieutenant that the best thing to be done, since no attack had been launched as yet, was to go back to camp where the porters were sleeping and waken them quietly. In the meantime one *askari* and myself would move silently and in shadow to where the noise had first been heard.

In absolute silence we all moved off according to plan.

The fear in our bellies belaboured our breathing. Every inhalation and exhalation roared in my ears and my heart drummed so loudly that I was convinced we would be compromised at any minute.

My comrade moved quietly behind me, taking care to place each step in the spoor I had left. We were crouched low, not wanting our silhouettes to show up against the slivers of night sky that in places pushed through the trees. We had gone only a few yards when I heard two distinct noises coming from my front-left, only five or six paces away. We lay flat on the ground, knowing full well that if we could hear them they could certainly hear us. To mask the noise we may have made I gave a faint owl hoot. It could well have been a rat or a mouse in the grass. We realized later that these actions had worked to our advantage as we had been mistaken for another section of the raiding party by the enemy.

We lay dead still in this position, straining our eyes, trying to penetrate the darkness, desperate to pick up the slightest movement, or perhaps a shape too bulky and out of place, but we saw nothing. A breeze blew up, causing a fair amount of rustling in the trees and the grass. Taking advantage of this we advanced a few more feet, our noise carried away under camouflage of the wind. Our enemy had obviously done the same thing, neither of us aware of the other's position and in their case, our presence.

It was while lying flat on the ground, partially hidden by some scrub, that I noticed—a very short distance from me—what appeared to be a tree trunk taking a step forward. Our position was precarious. Were we lying—half exposed, half concealed by the leaves and sagging branches of an immature shrub—on the outside of what was obviously an enemy party or were we in fact lying across their path? In this game of predator and prey it was difficult to decide what to do next and who would in fact make the next move.

I resolved that it would be best to lie perfectly still and allow events to take their course as it was quite impossible to know what their next move would be. Of small consolation was that they clearly had no idea we were there. We did not have to wait long and they passed us, moving slowly in the direction of the camp. It was fortunate that we were on their extreme flank, meaning their leader was probably in the middle of the group. Through careful observation I was able to discern the movement of four people. As a warning to my comrade I tapped him gently four times with my foot, indicating that I had seen the source of our concern.

We didn't know how our sentry had been captured or where they had taken him. We were by now some twenty paces from the campfire, far from his designated beat. As I saw the enemy moving I slowly stood up. Their footfall became our footfall, each step perfectly in time. They moved toward the fire and we followed, in line, behind them. As I managed to get closer I was able to position myself in a manner that silhouetted them against the fire. I counted seven in total.

We were now ten paces from the fire and it was becoming crucial that we take some sort of immediate action. The element of surprise was on our side and we would need to use this to our best advantage, forcing the surprised gang to run directly into the battle-ready arms of the lieutenant or else clear off into the darkness. Soundlessly, using slow hand movements I indicated to the *askari* beside me that our first strike would be at the two men in the centre of the gang. We would bayonet them in the back, then swing around, him to the left and me to the right, turn and shoot the men on either side. Our aim would need to be keen and careful. The lieutenant would almost certainly have taken the porters and other *askaris* into the bush-line on the other side of

Mzee Ali

the fire. The gunshots in the still night air would raise the alarm among our men and we would have to drop to the ground as soon as we had finished our attack, giving the lieutenant and his men a chance to fire in the direction of the commotion.

That was our plan and we quickly made up the ground between the gang of Wagogo. Making as little noise as possible, each marking his man, we were soon behind our initial targets. Almost immediately the two men tried to turn and fight us off but their reactions were slow, so stunned were they by our presence. We wasted no time thrusting the cold metal of our bayonets into their kidneys—my left hand gripping the left shoulder of my victim, pulling him onto me, while the right delivered the deadly blow. Then one final thrust, deeper into the man's belly. Pushing him away the bayonet slid out easily. No sooner had they dropped to the ground than we swung round and shot the two men on either side of us. Stab, shoot and fall to ground, no more than half a minute had passed. It was dark and our movements so quick that it was difficult to say whether our aim had been accurate. But it was enough to cause the rest of the gang to scatter. The men to the left, wary of escaping to the front because of the light of the fire, fled instead to our left. The lieutenant had noted the position of our firing and waited just long enough for the two fleeing warriors to be clear of our position, without his fire jeopardizing our safety. The calculated precision of his attack was remarkable and no sooner had he established our position than he and his men opened fire on the two fleeing Wagogo. Though their aim was not true because of the darkness and the number of rounds so rapidly fired, both men fell heavily to the ground. The warriors who had cleared off to my right were gone. Whether they had been hit or not we did not know but with the gang having now dispersed we called to the lieutenant. With adrenalin pumping and rifles at the ready it was necessary for us to reveal our position, let him know we were safe and were making our way toward him.

The fire was stoked into a crackling blaze and we reported back to the lieutenant. There were the two men we had bayoneted, the two who had fled to the left and the two who had fled to the right, which left one unaccounted for as I had originally counted seven.

The lieutenant issued his orders. We were to gather brands of grass, light them and search the bush in the vicinity of the camp. We found the first two almost immediately, shot through the chest, killed by the lieutenant and his men. Not ten paces from their bodies lay another man, shot through the hip. He was no doubt the man my fellow *askari* had shot. Then we came across the two men we had bayoneted—alive and still writhing on the ground. A badly injured kidney would not kill them for a couple of days, but the pain was excruciating and they would start to drift in and out of consciousness before eventually dying from loss of blood. Our safari was a small, tight unit and we did not have the capacity to forfeit four men to carry wounded captives. No discussion took place. We stood and watched for a moment or so, each with his own thoughts, knowing the lieutenant would issue his instructions in due course. I watched his expressionless face as he deliberately withdrew his revolver and with a single bullet each to the head, dispatched both.

We had yet to find our sentry, but there was little hope of finding him alive. We formed an extended line and swept through the immediate vicinity of the camp but our search was fruitless. We retraced our steps, but this time spreading out farther from the camp. A short sharp yell from a man to my right brought us all running. At first, he thought a snake had bitten him but it turned out to be the sharp edge of a bayonet, lying discarded on the ground—our sentry's bayonet. I suggested we were looking too close to the perimeter of the camp and should search farther afield. The bayonet was lying in such a position as to suggest that it pointed to the sentry's whereabouts. Had he been approached from the front, he would probably have fired off a shot. The Wagogo had almost certainly surprised him and taken him from behind, before dragging him away to be murdered.

We found him eventually, stripped naked. It was a gruesome sight—his stomach had been ripped open, his entrails spilled in a pulpy mess around him. His tongue had been cut out and his manhood severed and shoved into his mouth. Some of the men turned away, the horror of such brutality too much to contemplate, while others simply stood and stared, eyes vacant. On closer examination it appeared that some of his stomach parts had been completely removed, no doubt to be used as medicine for witchcraft. No one turned to look when the sounds of retching came from behind a nearby bush. There are times when a man must be allowed his privacy, free of pity or judgment.

We collected his body and took it back to camp. One of the porters was instructed by the lieutenant to sew up his stomach.

The breaking of pink light before dawn took us by surprise. We had not realized how the night's hours had been devoured by this encounter. Somehow the light made it all the less awful and, as the porter worked to restore the corpse to some dignity, so our minds were able to tuck this episode away and we breathed easier.

We buried the *askari* with his blankets in the pale light. The ceremony was short, as we had neither the time nor the facilities for a proper burial. The grave was piled high with soil, indicating its position in the middle of the African bush. The bodies of the raiding gang were stripped of what little they wore. The lieutenant kept such articles as souvenirs of the raid. Their bodies were left where they had fallen to be devoured by the beasts and birds of the forest.

We settled down to rest until sunrise. As dawn broke the cook-boy boiled coffee for the lieutenant and us ten *askaris*. The warm drink revived us, after which we formed up in marching order and, on the lieutenant's command, moved forward once again on our march to the coast.

Naturally our progress that day was sluggish and we were able to cover only a short distance. That night we simply slept in the bush near neither water nor amenity. We lived like this for a further three days. As we passed water points we filled our bottles and goatskins and moved on.

Eventually we arrived at the settlement of Morogoro. Here we met up with two other German teams, one that had left Tabora many months before on a general survey, much as we had done from Tabora to Kigoma. The other had made its way inland from Dar es Salaam.

Here at Morogoro the lieutenant received orders not to proceed farther until the main body joined him, on its way with the company commander from Tabora. We were grateful for the break, as we had faced considerable hardship on our journey. Our trials were soon forgotten though. Morogoro's lively atmosphere absorbed us. There were so many things to do that we were soon refreshed and unburdened. We waited ten days for the main body to join us. There was great excitement at the reunion, equally for the Europeans as with us. Everyone had a story and tales of the adventures were told and re-told, some elaborated upon to such an extent that they resembled ancient myths told to children at bedtime. But we enjoyed every one of them, laughing and celebrating together.

We rested a further three days and then proceeded on what had by now become a fairly well-worn route to Dar es Salaam. During this three-week-long trek we came across the first motorcars ever to have been brought to Tanganyika. Needless to say these were quite a phenomenon to all the Africans of the hinterland. We stared and joked, jostled about together, our wonder tempered with not a little bit of trepidation. It was beyond our comprehension how such a mass of steel and iron could move around on four wheels with a European sitting inside it. It appeared that it moved by his command. At no time did he take his hands off a fifth wheel, inside the machine, that was connected to the body by means of a steel rod. Moving this wheel appeared to direct the movements of this peculiar monster. On the whole it made a lot of noise, which we put down to some strange and unexplained form of European witchcraft.

Sixteen days later we arrived in Dar es Salaam and there, surely, we beheld for the first time the true fascination of European civilization. Roads were being built, with trucks carrying heavy loads moving this way and that. Concrete wharves were being constructed in the bay so that great ships with enormous cargoes of steel, engines, and many other things too numerous and too incomprehensible to mention, could dock and off-load their goods with giant cranes that reached into the sky. It was all too much to take in but slowly, as we came to understand the workings of these noisy machines, I suppose we grew accustomed to them and started to understand their purpose.

It was electricity, however, that stole our imaginations and wonder. How something that could not be seen pass through wires, that could produce light by pressing a switch, was beyond us. We sat for many hours in wonderment, clicking the switches on and off, on and off—until the lieutenant angrily came and told us this was a dangerous practice.

It was in this air of change and novelty and wonder that we settled, not knowing what job we would be called upon to do next or what other revelation of European invention would astound us.

It was while in Dar es Salaam that I first came across prostitution, the practice of which was introduced by the scarcity of European women. Previously, prostitution was unknown, because we either had as many wives as we wished for in accordance with the laws of Islam, or we had slave girls who were no more than concubines. Such women, therefore, did not willingly sell their bodies to strangers or any other person. They were entirely for the use of their owners. So willingly selling one's body was a foreign concept to us.

One night, while I was out with some of my friends in the village near the military barracks, we observed a number of

European men making their way down the street to a nearby hut where it was commonly known that *pombe* (beer) was frequently made. To my friends and me *pombe* was a forbidden beverage but we were curious to know why so many Europeans were visiting this particular house. We followed them in and were accosted by an elderly woman who appeared to be a freed slave. She offered us a drink but we declined and said that we were merely there for entertainment. She let us pass and we found ourselves seats in the dark shadows at the back of the large room into which we had been led. The room smelt strongly of stale beer and sweat, the floor was rouge and the furnishings scarce. At one end the room was heavily lit by candles and it was here that a number of white men sat drinking *pombe*. It was clear from their raised voices and joviality that they had been there for some time. We shifted around uncomfortably, but our curiosity was stronger than our desire to leave so we waited, trying to disappear into the shadows cast against the wall by the candles. In hushed tones we tried to determine the purpose of this place. There were many decent places where these men could go and drink, even local beer, so why would they come to this dingy out-of-the-way house? We each took our turn in surmising the answers and were still busy dreaming up the most imaginative reasons when the old woman reappeared. She went over to the group of men and talked to them, gesticulating with her hands as she spoke. After an animated conversation it seemed there was general approval among the men over whatever it was that she had suggested. This was all most intriguing so we decided to wait a while longer and see what happened.

She went through a back door and after a short while came back, followed by a number of young girls, probably no older than about fourteen. The girls were naked save a small form of G-string. As they came trooping into the room they started dancing. The dance was so suggestive that its only purpose could have been to arouse the men for whom they danced. Their firm bosoms vibrated fiercely in time to the song they chanted, their feet shuffling rhythmically, their bottoms jerking, with the candles throwing warped, disfigured shadows across the room. I had seen young girls dance before. Perhaps in other times their dancing could even have been construed as provocative, but this left little to the imagination. It was different, even degrading. Nothing was left to the imagination, their message as clear as the intentions of the salivating men at the counter. The rolling movements of their hips and buttocks were conducted with sexuality rather than sensuality. Regardless, one could not but desire to take one of them. Everything was there on display—their physical beauty, their agility, their youth—and displayed in such a manner so as only to highlight each of these sensuous qualities. Occasionally, their dancing would bring them close to the men who would fumble around, reaching with greedy fingers in an effort to touch them. But the girls had obviously been trained well and slipped easily from their probes without seeming to brush them off, but rather to further entice them.

This game continued for a while and eventually one of the girls allowed one of the men a brush of his hand across her bottom, another a finger over a pert nipple. At this stage the old woman stepped forward and demanded a sum of money from the men.

From our shadows we able to see that each man happily handed over a five-heller note. Once the woman was paid she clapped her hands two or three times and the dancing girls approached the men, still vibrating their bodies so as not to break the atmosphere of desire they had so craftily created. Each man stood and grappled to embrace his girl, clumsily pushing his chest up against the breasts of his prize. The girls squirmed to free themselves before leading their respective men away to tiny, dark, box-type rooms behind the room where we sat, astounded. There they would undress their man and give him the satisfaction he had purchased.

Once they had left we were able to talk to the old woman and discovered that the money she collected in exchange for the girls' bodies was used to feed and clothe them and to contribute to whatever she could do to look after them.

During that summer when we discovered prostitution we had no idea how it would grow and spawn into one of the greatest evils of our land. That was the price demanded for the wonders of European development.

We stayed in Dar es Salaam for another three months before being called upon to start on construction of the Dar es Salaam–Kigoma railway line, a vast task that would consume many years … and many lives.

XII

There were two tasks to be completed. The concrete wharves in the port had to be built for the ships to berth and off-load their goods and the first tracks of the cross-country railway line had to be laid. It was the taming of wild Tanganyika.

The construction of a railway line through country previously traversed only on foot is not an easy job. The procedure itself is complex and laborious, not to mention the challenges the land itself imposed on the project.

Thousands upon thousands of sleepers of local timber were sawn by machines into set lengths and sizes. The ground on which these were to be laid first had to be packed with stones. These stones had to be broken up by hand with hammers and then carried in *kararias* (large metal basins) and dumped on the survey line. Other gangs would then level the mounds of stone and stamp them solidly into the ground. On the packed stone the sleepers were laid at measured distances and over these the railway line was then laid, held in place by big iron nails. At every length of railway line a small gap was left before the next line was laid. We later learned that this was to allow for the expansion of metal that took place in the heat of the sun.

After the initial two weeks of laying the line we started moving beyond the outskirts of Dar es Salaam. There were many, many thousands of Africans employed in this work. In the front was the survey gang that pegged the line, followed by the cutting gang, which consisted of labourers whose job it was to cut down all the trees along the line of survey pegs for a distance of twenty yards on either side. A labour force, responsible for levelling ground and construction of culverts and small bridges, followed. Next came the stone-layers, who packed and consolidated the stone on the levelled ground, ready for the sleeper gang that positioned the timber sleepers. They, in turn, were followed by the track-laying gang, with all followed closely by the supply train that carried all the materials needed for the progress of the line.

No real problems were encountered during the first few weeks but soon we were faced with having to build up large earthen embankments and construct bridges to cross lengthy depressions in the ground and, of course, rivers. This was a heavy task which, over the following months, would have to be repeated many times. The earth was excavated by hand a short distance from the survey line, carried on labourers' heads in *kararais* and then dumped in the area where the line would run. It was ceaseless, thankless hard work, day in and day out. Thousands upon thousands of loads of soil had to be dug, carried to the dumping point, packed and consolidated, before any stones or sleepers could be laid.

The survey gangs were moving ahead quickly but construction was slow. Camping huts were built out of whatever was available to us. Here we slept and ate, day after exhausting day. There was no respite or time-off; the work had to go on. Our German masters supervised at all times. Beatings were meted out to men thought to be dragging their heels. The Germans would bellow instructions from the time the second rooster crowed until we fell broken to the ground at the end of each day, with enough energy only to eat and lie down. We resented them. They wanted a railway line and we had to build it while they walked alongside, yelling and cursing, finding fault in many of our efforts. Looking back I suppose that their constant watch and supervision, their efficiency and dogged attitude, is what finished the line—that was their expertise.

And so we inched forward, sleeper by painful sleeper, until we reached the dense forest areas, infested with tsetse fly and game. Sickness was taking its toll and we stuck to our age-old practice of taking the sick or dying out into the bush to be left to their fates. Large numbers of men were dealt with in this way and thus the numerous predators in the area became accustomed to the taste of human flesh, the quick meal. They became accustomed to our presence and learned not to fear us, but rather to take advantage of the easy feed.

It was while in this wild area that we had our first brush with man-eating lions, so turned by our own hand. Work had stopped for the day and men were sitting, quietly chatting around their fires, swapping stories, having a dig at one of the Germans, or laughing at a particularly tall tale. From one of the fires four men got up to go and relieve themselves in the surrounding bush before going to sleep. Suddenly from the direction they had gone, the all-too-familiar screams of men in anguish rang out. Through the din I could hear that they were trying to call out something but it was impossible to discern the words. A number of us grabbed our spears and lighting brands and ran in their direction. We came across one man, on his hands and knees, crawling, his innards dragging in the dirt beneath him. He was trying to shout out something but all he could do was gurgle. The flesh on his back had been ripped open, his ribs visible through the claw marks. His shoulder had been bitten clean through and his face was severely lacerated. In this state he had been trying to escape from his attackers—obviously lion.

The news spread like a locust plague through the camp and the atmosphere turned in an instant from a tired murmur to anxious chatter. Some of the Germans were informed about what had happened and they grabbed their rifles and arrived on the scene. But there was nothing anybody could do. The darkness and density of the bush in the vicinity prohibited any action. The injured man was taken to the hospital tent, while the rest of us, flaming torches in hand, tried to find the other three missing men. All we found were smears of blood and the occasional piece of torn clothing. We tried to follow the spoor but the uncertainty of the light made it impossible to find the other victims. There was some concern that they might return in an attempt to find the injured man.

Six of us were given rifles and told to lie in wait for their possible return.

We sat back to back close to the scene and in that way we faced every possible direction and were thus less likely to be taken by surprise. The rest were told to go back to camp and maintain extreme silence. After a short while, in the deadly silence that had descended on the area, the sound of bones being crunched and heavy breathing drifted toward us from a short way off. We decided to split up—three would stay and the others would go and investigate the noise. Carefully, with lighted brands, we moved in the direction of the grisly sound. The terror was in not knowing how many lions there were or their exact position. After advancing some sixty paces in the general direction of the noise, it stopped. We were now in grave danger. For all we knew there could be an entire pride of lions, for which three bodies would not be a sufficient meal, thereby making us their next target. We were shifting forward slowly when a distinct noise came from our front, offset slightly to my left. We were afraid and we had no idea what we were up against. With this in mind it was decided that the best course of action would be to fire a volley of shots in the direction of the noise. Following the crash of rifle-fire there was a flurry of movement in the bush, and then, complete silence.

We hoped to retrieve some of the remains of the three victims. Within a short distance we found the remains of one. Between the first screams and our volley of rifle-fire the lions had managed to eat all but a piece of his leg, a hand and his head. No other remains, of any bodies, were found.

We handed the grisly remains over to the Germans. The man was identified and his remains placed in a sack to be buried the following morning. Instructions were issued that no man was to leave the campsite, not for any reason whatsoever. A double shift of guards was instituted and a line of fires was lit on the perimeter. In this manner the camp was kept in relative peace for the remainder of the night.

Early the following morning the camp commandant with a

number of *askaris* proceeded to the spot where the remains of the men killed during the night had been found. We searched a while for any other remains but found only bits of bone, skin and hair. The spoor of the man-eaters was picked up and followed.

It led away from the camp towards a *mishito*, a water-hole, at the headwaters of a small stream some four miles from the camp and leading in a direction away from the construction site. Tracking was not difficult since much of the grass in the area had been burned. The depressions left by the lions' paws were quite clear in the burned ash of the grass. We had to be careful though because the spoor passed by smaller clumps of scrub and patches of unburned grass, where the killer-lions could quite easily have been hiding, waiting in ambush.

The camp commandant and two other Europeans with rifles followed the lead tracker, with a number of *askaris* in the rear. Our progress was slow, not because of our numbers—we were all well-trained, agile men—but we had no desire to stumble upon the lions as a result of carelessness.

However, there was no sign of the beasts until we reached the vicinity of the *mishito*. It was obvious that they had made their way to the water-hole to drink after gorging themselves on the flesh of our companions. It appeared that the pride consisted of at least five animals, probably an older male, a lioness and three three-quarter-grown cubs. The danger was that these cubs had now learned to enjoy the flesh of humans and understood what easy prey they were.

On nearing the *mishito* the tracker indicated that the lions were definitely very close. The spoor led into the *mishito* and then out again, encircling the area around the water-hole. Now we had to be very quiet, each movement calculated and measured, as the slightest noise would alert them. Lions are by nature lazy. If disturbed, they would move from their sleeping places to positions deep in the heart of the dense bush adjacent to the stream. It would be difficult to reach them there, as progress would be impossible in the impenetrable undergrowth.

We had followed the spoor round the *mishito* for some fifty or sixty paces when a low rumble from the edge of a thicket warned the tracker and the commandant that we had found them.

A plan of attack now had to be devised in such a way that at no time would any member of the party be exposed to the danger of crossfire. An immediate decision had to be made on the tactics we would employ. The lions had seen us and would be starting to slink away.

Our instructions were that one European and some of the *askaris* would run as fast as possible to the stream, maintaining a distance of some twenty-five paces from the edge of the forest. After about a hundred and fifty yards they were to cut through the undergrowth towards the stream. Another section of the party were to retrace our original steps and take up positions on the other side of the stream. In that way they would be able to fire downstream without risk of their fire hitting any of their comrades on the other side of the river. Should the lions cross the stream there would be little chance of the first team coming directly into the line of fire.

We were given a couple of minutes to get into position. The commandant then moved forward with his men to the point where the growling had been heard. He left two men behind as a stopgap between himself and the first party in case the animals tried to make good their escape and slip away through the two parties. The tension was tangible. There was no telling what would happen over the course of the next few minutes—the viciousness of a cornered lion cannot be matched by any other wild animal.

The lions had not moved. Whether they had stayed out of curiosity or whether waking them from their lazy slumber had incited them, was impossible to say. However, when the commandant and his men approached the lair the lions decided to move off downstream, as we had hoped. Cautiously the commandant maintained his pursuit. He and his men had now left the relative safety of the open and were penetrating deeper and deeper into the forest. Their vulnerability increased with each step, each footfall marred by the snapping of twigs and crunching of leaves. Visibility in the partial light and thick vegetation was so poor that they had to stop every few paces and strain their eyes and ears to pick up the trail. It was while standing quite still in the hazy light, with every sense, every nerve-ending on edge, that the commandant heard the first shot. It had come from the direction of the first team. The lions had moved fast; they must have been at least a hundred yards ahead.

The lions now broke ranks and split up, each moving according to instinct and that was when the trouble started. To track a pride is one thing, but to track five individual lions is impossible. It was now up to each one of us to rely on our instincts too. The lions had taken their cover, individually, invisible to us.

During my years in the bush I had learned that, as animals have different calls for different occasions, so too do men. A scream of shocked terror is one I was fast able to discern among any other cry, be it for help or any other purpose.

The simultaneous scream of an *askari* and rifle-fire from the right flank set off a wave of panic through the rest of the men and many ran to his assistance. He had been crouched low in sparse cover doing as we all were, trying to see the target through the foliage before it saw us. They had seen each other at the same time, the lioness and him. He screamed and fired and she charged. As she leaped at him the bullet struck, but it did not stop her and she landed heavily on top of him, pinning him to the ground. Her pain must have registered for she retreated, but not before severely mauling her victim. The remaining *askaris* started firing at random and in all directions, abandoning all training, all strategy and all sense. In the ensuing chaos it was impossible to tell what was actually happening. The firing continued for two or three more minutes and then stopped abruptly. The shrill, sharp whistle of the commandant summoned us to him. During the report-back we learned that three lions had been shot during the indiscriminate firing, leaving two unaccounted for. It was essential that we find and destroy them.

Two *askaris* had been mauled by the enraged lioness, with one critical and in great pain. His legs had been badly bitten, he had been partially disembowelled by the tearing action of her hind legs as she'd landed on him, his right ear had been ripped off and his shoulder was a bloody mess. Water was fetched from the stream so that first aid could be administered.

Three *askaris* were ordered to pick up the trail of the wounded lioness.Flecks of blood on blades of grass led away from the stream towards a number of anthills, densely covered in bush. Approaching one such anthill, the three men realized that not only were they facing a lioness angered by her wounds but one that had been separated from her cubs, the latter condition infinitely more threatening. Her behaviour would be completely unpredictable— she might charge or she might lure them deeper into the thicket, restricting their movements and giving her the advantage of ambush. The German accompanying the *askaris* took up position some fifty yards from the anthill. He instructed the other men to move round the anthill in a wide berth, and attempt to drive her out by making as much commotion as possible. Her growls could be heard quite distinctly from the midst of the bush and as long as she kept this up her exact position remained known to the pursuers. Once in position the men began shouting and beating branches, desperately trying to make as much noise as possible so as to frighten her into breaking cover and giving the German a clear shot. But she did not break cover—she was trapped and saw the forest as her only protection. Desperate to retreat farther she charged the men, catching them completely off guard. Her first target dropped his rifle and he was only able to keep her strong jaws from savaging him by gripping frantically at her throat, her blood now flowing steadily from the wound in her side. Lion and man grappled like this for some minutes, each fighting desperately for survival.

The other men shouted out their position and aimed their rifles at the lioness, firing directly into her shoulder. This enraged her further and, while keeping her first assailant pinned down, she swung to face her attackers. Her body was weakening fast and her fury alone could no longer save her. The *askaris* re-loaded and put a bullet in her head.

The brutalized victim was helped to his feet and half-dragged to the commandant. Thus four out of the five lions had been killed and we presumed that by now the fifth had escaped to safer hunting grounds.

The injured men were carried back to camp on crudely constructed *mashilas*. Two men were left to guard the dead animals. In due course the commandant sent out a detail of labourers to fetch them. On seeing the carcasses there was a great ovation from the men in the camp. These lions had killed and completely devoured two men, critically injured two and wounded a further three.

The beasts were skinned and buried in the ground to rot.

XIII

After this incident camp life returned to relative normality. Overseers and labour gangs were increased. Machinery for construction of embankments, cutting trees, excavation of cuttings and many other heavy jobs, arrived.

Prison gangs were introduced to supplement the construction teams. These people were classed as being 'un-free' as they had been committed to sentences of punishment for various misdemeanours. They were looked upon with contempt by the hired gangs and treated severely by their guards. They were kept isolated from the rest of us in camp and, in addition to a normal day's hard labour, had to attend to the cleanliness of the camp. In fact, they were generally considered slaves by all and sundry.

Although the rest of us all performed the same backbreaking work on the construction of the line, these men had to work even harder. Not because they had more work to do but because they were shown little mercy by the Germans—that any deviation no matter how minor would have them publicly flogged. One too many sips of water, standing straight for a moment to ease the pain burning in their lower backs, even just glancing up at a passing guard, was construed as disobedience. In the old days we flogged slaves, made examples of them. Times had not changed—

only the people who meted out the punishment. It seemed not to matter whether the man being flogged was young or old, weak or strong. He was to be an example, not only to the other prisoners, but also to us. We would all have to gather round, barely able to stand ourselves and watch a broken man being beaten, over and over and over again.

The railway line from Dar es Salaam to Kigoma is literally built upon the blood, sweat and tears of many thousands of men. There was no reprieve, no let-up and never, not once, a slackening in discipline.

And so life continued. It was not good to focus on the distance that lay ahead—that would destroy a man's spirit—you had to simply keep your head down, your heart strong and think only about that particular rock, or tree, or sleeper.

Some eight days after the lion hunt we learned that one of the men injured during the hunt had died. The other men in the camp hospital, still struggling for their lives, were removed and sent back to Dar es Salaam for better treatment.

Though women and children were few in the camps, the first we knew of the re-appearance of the lion was when a young child was carried away from the outskirts of the camp early one afternoon. But as the labour was all out at work and the Europeans busy supervising, the disappearance was not noticed until much later. Again we were called upon to assist in tracking the beast, but all we were able to find was a small head and a foot. This caused much speculation in the camp and around each campfire at night discussions were centred on the possibility of the lion having imbued the spirit of a human.

The lion's cunning seemed beyond the normal understanding of a wild beast. He appeared to have a sixth sense directing him whenever he made an attack on any stray member of camp. As the camp moved forward with the advance of the construction, he followed, striking with uncanny certainty whenever he felt the pangs of hunger. His courage grew with time—which in the end proved his downfall. It was his habit to hide in the darkness, watching the movements of sentries and others. When, in his estimation the time was ripe, he would stalk his prey from behind and soundlessly make his kill by immediately biting the base of the skull and thus paralyzing any scream, before dragging his victim away into the bush. Sometimes he would ambush a hut that did not appear to be as strongly constructed as the others. By charging at the door and knocking it down, he would enter the hut, grab a victim and make off with his prey into the bush.

The commandant refused to allow relatives to remove the remains of the savaged family members from the bush, hoping to lure the beast back and give him an opportunity to shoot it. This tactic failed utterly. By chance one day the commandant was out hunting with a number of others, when they accidentally walked straight into the lion's lair. The lion showed himself only momentarily as he dashed to another bush for better cover. They spotted him and simple orders were issued—the hunting party was to follow and kill him. This was accomplished with comparative ease since there was little other available cover to which he could escape. Seeing a brown patch in the grass, an officer fired at it. The bullet found its mark and the lion sprang out with a roar, only to collapse some ten paces from the officer, dead.

On examining the body it was found to have three scars, apparently old bullet wounds. This indicated that it was a member of the original pride that we had previously hunted down. The lion was carried back to camp and after it was skinned the commandant ordered its stomach be opened. We found pieces of copper wire, brass wire, beads and a few other items, proving beyond doubt that this was the very beast that had been plaguing us for these past weeks.

XIV

An advance party reported that we were only a matter of two days away from the Ngerengere River. This was a landmark in the construction of the railway line as it was comparatively the first major obstacle we had encountered. To us it seemed impossible that anything could be built across this river that would withstand the weight of the enormous machines—the trains with their many trucks and carriages. But these white men were not deterred. Harder and harder tasks were thrust on us to hasten our arrival at this landmark and we reached it a day and a half later, half a day ahead of schedule. The work involved in reaching the river was considerable, since mountainsides had had to be cut away in places and embankments built up in others, but at all times keeping the survey level of the line.

Building the bridge across the Ngerengere River was a major task. The trains brought up enormous girders of steel, which had to be lifted by crane, as they were too heavy to manhandle. The European engineers had enormous concrete foundations laid, onto which the foot girders were bolted. All work had to take place well above water level to make allowance for the flood periods. The span of the bridge had to be fashioned by riveting girders to each other, which then had to be manoeuvred into position by crane. On these girders were laid the wooden sleepers that in due course would support the tracks.

Many accidents occurred during this time—men were crushed under the weight of the girders—others, overly familiar with their tasks, would run along unsupported girders or sleepers, stumble and fall into the river below. There was no saving them. By the time the alarm had been raised crocodiles would have already taken them.

The rains came and we found ourselves floundering in mud and water. The Ngerengere River, which has its source many miles to the north in the hills towards Bagamoyo, had, however, shown no sign of rising, though there had been about four days of overcast, rainy weather.

One afternoon, a distant rumbling sound, like a far-off earthquake, reached our ears and our pulses beat a little faster. This work was not only about building a railway line—it was about conquering nature in order to build a railway line—slicing up her mountains, raising her valley floors, fording her rivers. And she wasn't taking this placidly. We had come to accept this and thus unfamiliar sounds or screaming struck every man to his core.

The construction engineer sent a team upstream in an effort to find the source of the noise. We never saw them again. The first we were to see of the coming peril was a wall, eight or so feet high, of reeds, trees and mud descending upon the construction site, engulfing all in its path. I had never seen anything like it. I had seen flooding before where waters rose and rose, but never anything like this. This flood had started at the source of the river, thus it had gained considerable momentum, wiping out everything in its path and carrying it along—a monster consuming everything in its way—plant, animal and human alike. There was no telling what effect it would have on the bridge and what would happen when it burst its banks. The pylons in the river would cause a damming effect, bottle-necking the water and compounding the pressure. It was moving at about ten paces a minute, bearing all before it.

Panic took on a new meaning and it was instant. It did not grow slowly as the wave of death approached; it ignited in every man as one. At that particular moment many labourers were digging foundations in the riverbed and many craftsmen were atop the bridge. And still it raged—the closer it came the more debris it carried with it. Many upstream who were camped close to the river found themselves swamped under grass, mud and water, their huts seemingly made of paper. Their efforts to withstand its power were fruitless and they and their belongings were swept away and churned up with the rest of the debris. Pandemonium ensued.

The engineers were desperately trying to save the bridge, the German officers were desperately trying to restore order and the labourers were desperately trying to save themselves.

Orders and instructions yelled by voices themselves edged in hysteria—fell on deaf ears. I learned that day, under circumstances such as these, that a man's true character shows itself to the world. And it is not always something one would like to bear witness to. Save yourself, at any cost.

The trench foundations we were digging were deep and difficult to get out of at the best of times. The past few days' rain had made the sidewalls slippery and treacherous. Scrambling men managed to haul themselves out and then simply disappeared. One man was reaching back to help his fellow workers when he caught a glimpse of the monster behind him—he looked back into the trench, his eyes wide, shame and guilt and confusion etched into his face. Another quick look over his shoulder and he ran without so much as another glance at the men pleading for help, men he had been working with, side by side, every day for months on end … comrades.

It is in times like this when man's animal nature rears its head—that nature which is ordinarily suppressed by our everyday niceties. Survival is king.

As I stood on the banks, trying to make sense of instructions being barked down at me from the bridge, I too glanced upstream to see how much time we had. I noticed a man fleeing his home. The hut was already knee-deep in water, the trunk of a tree blocking the doorway. A young child was trapped behind the tree inside the house. She was screaming at her father, arms raised imploringly. The child shrieked again as the body of her mother washed up beside her, with her mother's head jamming up against the tree. The child was hysterical. Once free from the massive obstacle blocking the doorway he waded away, struggling through the mud and reeds that were wrapping themselves around his legs. He didn't so much as look back as his child, his flesh and blood, stood wailing, now chin-deep in the floodwaters.

When the floodwaters struck the bridge they hit with such a force that the men still scrambling to escape were thrown clear—

some were immediately gathered up into the deluge and others tossed headlong into the river below. Astoundingly, the bridge seemed the only obstacle able to withstand the fantastic force, but in its defiance pylons were channelling the rolling debris into deadly torrents that raged through the gaps between the pillars and the embankment. Two uncompleted pillars collapsed in an instant, like straw.

Nightfall did not bring with it any calm. Panic prevailed as furiously as the waters. It was difficult to light fires as the wood was soaked through. The night sky hung low with cloud and permitted little moon or starlight. In the darkness we fumbled around in an attempt to restore some semblance of order and attend to the injured.

It was impossible to calculate, or even estimate, the damage the flood had caused, or the number of lives lost. During impromptu roll calls, many names were called and the response was silence. The Germans had taken to using *sjambok* (whips of hippo hide) to restore order among the labourers and it appeared to be working.

On the following day the river was still raging and no further work could be done on the bridge until the water levels had subsided. We were able to ascertain that damage to the bridge had been considerable. Although it still stood, steel girders were grotesquely twisted, freshly laid concrete had been completely washed away and much valuable material had been lost.

The campsite was re-positioned on higher ground to avoid a repetition of the disaster.

As the water levels dropped so life at the site slowly returned to normal. Engineers realized that much of the work they had done had been in vain. Observing the height of the flood levels it was obvious that the bridge and its embankments were too low and would have to be re-built, far higher. As a result we worked at the river for a further three weeks. New and bigger pillars had to be constructed and girders re-positioned. Safety nets were hung in place from the ironwork of the bridge to prevent workers falling into the river below.

It was a great day when the last girder was positioned and riveted home. Sleepers were laid and again the trains chugged forward, carrying the construction materials. That bridges could support such enormous loads, without collapsing or showing the slightest sign of strain, was indeed a feat of wonderment.

The line continued through the forests and across arid, hostile country. Malaria, sleeping sickness, typhoid and blackwater fever claimed scores of lives, African and European alike.

The weeks passed, the months passed. We reached Morogoro, crossed the flatlands of Dodoma, always in a westerly direction, until, at last, we reached Tabora in the country of the Wanyamwezi—the People of the Moon.

XV

Tabora had grown and was bursting with activity. Teams of engineers were surveying the final line to Kigoma and, as had been previously decided, a line to Mwanza on the shores of Lake Mwanza, also known as Lake Victoria by the British.

Many of us who were originally from Tabora were given a period of leave. We were able to take off our uniforms and return to the villages of our childhood. Yet this was not the Tabora of our childhood—the horizon had been obscured by the construction of many modern houses. Our pole and dagga huts looked insignificant and insecure against the massive structures of stone and concrete. But these huts were our homes and in them lay the essence of our family happiness.

Sitting around the small fires over which the family meal simmered, in the company of friends, we reminisced of the days before the Europeans had set foot in this land of ours. We spoke of our childhoods, the games we had played, our stories rooted in a deep melancholy, knowing our children would not grow up as we had. We spoke of the kraals we had built of poles and mud that housed our sheep and cattle. Livestock had denoted our wealth back then—now a man's status and wealth was determined by rank and colour and paper money.

So deep was our reverie that the spluttering and boiling of the meal went quite un-noticed, for which we were severely reprimanded by the women, however, an over-cooked meal paled in comparison to the trials we had experienced since the coming of the Germans. The horrors and exhausting work we had overcome in the past months replaced the problems of before and we brushed aside their complaints as trivial, a minor incident in the face of the present changes and this new world. At that stage I believed that nothing could ever compare to what we had been through, but I was to be proven wrong. Very wrong.

We ate in the company of women and children, our spirits lifted by the laughter and gaiety provoked by those with the skill to embellish a story, and draw it out with the tallest of tales. It was these stories that we held dear, stories of companionship and tomfoolery. They kept our hearts warm and our minds focused and clear. The cooking pots had long been removed, but still we sat around our fires, talking. There was nothing now to break the pictures framed by the fires. As the flames burned down to embers and the chill of the night air replaced its warmth and comfort so our storytelling and reminiscence died away too.

We spent our leave hunting and visiting friends, returning to the German camp from time to time to seek the latest news of progress on the railway line, to ascertain how much leave was still due, and what tasks lay ahead. Tomorrow was another day and while we had our leisure time we would make the most of it and enjoy it to the full.

And so our leave passed and again we found ourselves falling in on parade to the call of bugles. We stayed in Tabora, in camp, for another few weeks before being assigned as a protection unit to a team of railway engineers who were undertaking a reconnaissance of the route to Mwanza and the lake.

In the company of a number of Europeans, some five hundred labourers and a company of African *askaris*, we left Tabora behind. This was the first official expedition to cover the route of the future line to Mwanza. On the first day we covered some fifteen miles before making camp. The locals in this area were accustomed to the Germans and hastened to supply us with considerable amounts of food, produced as gifts—grain for us and chickens for the Germans. We welcomed these gifts as they saved our own food stocks.

To the west, only a few miles away, was the spot where Chief Mirambo had routed an army of Arabs in the early days when they had attacked him and his village. The Germans had heard of this battle and a number were interested in visiting the reported site. So a small company of us diverted to see if there were any visible remnants of the battle. Game in the area was plentiful and the safari was ordered to strike camp and proceed to a water point not far from the Gombe River. We pitched camp and spent a few days replenishing our food supplies.

During this time we were able to take the Germans to the glade of palm trees situated in a slight depression. This was the site of the battle where Mirambo had stood against the Arabs. He had ambushed the Arabs among these very palm trees, interspersed with numerous other wild trees and long grass. The Arab contingent had decided to attack Mirambo's village and annihilate him, yet when they arrived they found it completely deserted with little left to plunder. Thinking they had won a great victory, they started back to Tabora. Inflated by this perceived victory discipline in the ranks slackened on the return journey. Mirambo and his warriors, spearmen and archers, lay in wait for them in the glade. Only a few Arabs were able to escape through the dense foliage. This was also where the white man, Stanley, had been looking for Doctor Livingstone. He'd accompanied the Arabs and was fortunate enough to escape Mirambo's onslaught and survive. Old human bones and skulls were scattered around the area, no doubt victims of that great battle. The Germans showed considerable interest in our knowledge of the incident and made copious notes as we re-told the stories of old.

It was while camped here that three Germans and four of us *askaris* found ourselves in the middle of a large herd of elephants. The first we knew of our true position within the herd was when a European shot an elephant standing close by. At the sound of the shot the bush around us erupted with stampeding and trumpeting. We were out-numbered and surrounded. The elephants were furiously trampling and charging all about us. There was no one clear target we could shoot. The only solution was to take refuge next to the dead animal. We called the white men to join us and together we crouched low behind the fallen animal, its great bulk providing plenty of cover for the seven of us. Our cover was good and, given the situation, we were relatively safe. This was the kind of predicament that got men killed. Elephants take fright and try to escape, and in doing so they will trample anything in their path. We were out of their way and although they were still making an enormous amount of noise, they were moving off. They did so in a manner that appeared threatening, but to us their intentions were clear—they had picked up our scent and were endeavouring to get away. One of the Germans lost his nerve and discharged his firearm two or three times at the elephants. His foolishness did not immediately endanger us, but we did not know whether his bullets had found their mark and wounded any of the animals. This was cause for concern as we might yet cross the path of one of these injured beasts in days to come—a grave danger. Our immediate reaction was one of relief—at having escaped a possible stampede—but at the back of our minds the worry gnawed away. The officer in charge reprimanded the man who had so indiscriminately fired his rifle.

Although we were trained *askaris* and had served with the German East African Army for some time, our inherent belief in the ways of old was still prevalent. We insisted on carrying out the ritual afforded a slain elephant. The officer did not prevent us and after the ritual had been performed, two of us were sent back to camp to fetch labour to assist in cutting up the elephant and carrying the meat back to camp. Four or five days later we struck camp and rejoined the main body and continued towards Mwanza.

The country through which we passed was well wooded and in places very fertile. As we progressed westward our contact with civilization diminished and, after some three weeks of travelling, we entered the country of the Buha. They were an extremely primitive people, dignified but lacking in discipline. On entering the first Buha village we found it completely deserted with only a scattering of dogs and chickens to indicate any sign of life. We searched the huts and in one found a young child, obviously very ill. Our safari doctor examined her and pronounced her to be suffering from smallpox. This was undoubtedly the reason for the desertion. Among primitive peoples this was the most dreaded of all diseases.

The doctor immediately issued orders that every person on the safari who had not been vaccinated against the disease was to report for vaccination. To many, this was a most peculiar form of treatment—they had always believed there to be no cure. It was not long before the rumour was spreading, mostly among the labourers, that the Germans were using this case of smallpox as an excuse to sterilize the men. For this reason many of them refused vaccination. The Germans did not tolerate dissent of any kind whatsoever—this sort of refusal was absolutely unheard of. The commanding officer ordered the dissenters to be flogged. Orders were orders and disobedience would not be tolerated—that was that.

Two poles were cut from the bush and planted in an upright position, close enough together to tie up a man—his legs spread and each tied to a separate pole—his arms strapped in the same way, at the wrist, high above his head. The whole camp was paraded in front of the first dissident and armed *askaris* were posted around the labour force so that none would try and free the man. I was in charge of guarding those awaiting their flogging with instructions to shoot any man who tried to escape.

The first man, screaming and struggling against his restraints, was stripped naked. A German was detailed to take from the commandant's equipment a *sjambok* some seven feet long. He was to inflict no less than fifteen lashes across the man's back.

The man took his stance a little way to one side of the spread-eagled prisoner. He drew the *sjambok* behind him and with a side-sweep brought it across the man's back with a resounding crack. The pointed tip opened up the flesh where it made contact. The man's agonized cries did not deter his punisher who, after laying on some ten strokes, saw that the man's back was so lacerated that there was no untouched flesh available to accept further lashes. He completed the punishment with lashes across the man's buttocks. When it was done salt water was poured over the wounds to sterilize them and he was sent to the camp hospital to receive further treatment from the doctor.

He was unconscious when two *askaris* carried him off.

Each man who had refused vaccination was punished in the same way. Accordingly the whole camp was vaccinated.

Some of the villagers made a hesitant appearance, asking to be allowed back to their homes and, providing they bore no signs of the pox, were allowed to return, but not before they too had been vaccinated. Those bearing spots were stopped well before they reached the village and forced to return to the bush. They had a second option available to them—they could choose to be shot. News has an uncanny way of travelling well ahead of a safari and in many cases when we arrived at a village we found it deserted, all food and belongings having been removed by their owners. We lived on game meat, wild spinach and fruit.

We traversed some very harsh country, trekking across black-cotton soil where grew forests of tall trees, the thorns of which tore our clothing and made progress difficult, especially for the bare-footed porters.

But this was a vast and diverse country and the land gradually changed in character to undulating hills and savannah where low thorn trees grew, interspersed with big rocky outcrops. We knew we were nearing the shores of Lake Mwanza. The climate was changing from dry to moist, humid heat. We came across our first village overlooking the lake, ringed with numerous banana plantations. Fish from the lake was the staple diet of the local people and would provide us with a welcome change to the venison that had been our diet over the past weeks.

Topping the saddle of a range of hills we saw stretched to our left and right range upon range of rolling hills and, directly ahead, still some miles away, the vast waters of Lake Mwanza. After many months of battling with tsetse fly, hostile tribes and inhospitable, arid terrain it was surely a sight to behold. It was as if the setting sun dipping on the horizon had ignited the Bay of Mwanza into a flame, rising from the burning trunk of a tree. We camped there for the night and the following day, with flags flying to show that this was now German territory, we marched into Mwanza. We based up and awaited instructions.

XVI

At Mwanza we spent three weeks fishing and generally loafing around when orders came through that we were to return to Tabora immediately. This news was received with great joy as most of us had been away from home for quite some time. After a couple of days preparing for the return journey, the bugles blew and the company fell in on parade. So began the long march back. About a week out of Tabora we came across the railhead and, knowing many of the labourers, asked for news on the progress of the line to Kigoma, as well as news and tidings of friends and relatives left behind in Tabora.

Our stay at the railhead was short. We were put on the first train bound for Tabora. This was the first time any of us had been on a train and our excitement was boundless. Climbing into a carriage with all one's belongings and making camp in a moving steel box travelling at great speed was a novelty never to be forgotten and slow to pass. The noise was terrific. Great herds of game stampeded off into the bush at our passing, while others appeared to race the train. Men were hanging out the windows, shouting encouragement as though it were truly a race. However, some animals, stricken with panic, would dart across the tracks and meet an untimely death.

At last the train rolled into the station at Tabora and all we could do was stare in wide-eyed amazement at the transformation that had taken place during our absence. Great buildings, shunting yards, workshops and sheds had all been constructed. We disembarked and marched directly to the military camp to await orders.

Rumour was rife that we were to join the forward gangs building the stretch of line to Kigoma. Work had been held up at the crossing of the Malagaraise River.

The rumour proved to be true. In full military order we once again boarded the train, moving up to the construction gang at the head of the Kigoma line. As I said, it would be a while before the wonder of rail would lose its appeal, not only for us but also for the local villagers. They gathered in number to watch it slowly chug out of the station.

We disembarked at Usenge station, up to which point the line had been completed. In front of us the lines stretched ahead but as yet unconsolidated and therefore not safe to travel on.

It was late and we camped near the line that night, ready for an early start on the morrow. Tsetse flies were numerous and we heard of many cases of death and extreme illness but the Germans allowed nothing whatsoever to deter them from their task of finishing the line. It took two days to reach the Malagaraise station.

At the river there was great concern because the ground on which the embankment was being built for the crossing was too boggy. Every *kararia*-ful of earth laid on the boggy grond was merely swallowed up by the swamps on either side of the river. To combat this problem it was decided that the line should take a slight detour, passing through a range of hills bordering the swamps.

Here progress was fairly good until, once again, the actual river crossing had to be undertaken. The problem was that fantastically heavy material had to be transported across the river and then a team of workers on the other side had to build a solid embankment on the dryer ground verging the swampy edges of the river. This embankment had to provide sufficient foundation to be able to carry the weight of the steel bridge, as well as the weight of a train. The western embankment was to cover a distance of nearly a mile. It had to be built in a straight line, directly opposite the embankment on the eastern side of the river. The sheer magnitude of this task was quite unimaginable. There was great uncertainty as to the carrying capacity of the soil, thus vast quantities of rock and earth were required, far more than had ever been used before in any river crossing.

So many issues had to be taken into account. The great moving islands of papyrus upstream were of much concern, as they would be brought downriver during the floods in the rainy season. If the bridge were to have any mid-river supports it was more than likely that they would be washed away by the mass of papyrus and debris, exacerbated by the sheer volume of water.

So a single-span bridge, high enough for such islands of vegetation to pass under without obstruction, was decided upon.

Life was hard.

The men were tired and weak. The gruelling work, coupled with the mosquitoes, leeches, crocodiles and the relentless Germans, left many of them dead or dying.

Accidents were common, yet most of the time it was only those directly involved or working nearby who actually witnessed the tragedies. We would hear talk of them later around the campfires, the faces of the men impassive as they spoke. Whether trying to keep their emotions under strict control or immune to the everyday horrors, they gave nothing away—just the facts.

On one occasion I was close enough to witness a gang working on the far side of the river. They were trying to consolidate the embankment close to the water level. The man nearest the water found himself, quite unexpectedly, in the coils of a massive python, which was going about the business of wrapping itself around the man's body, working up from his legs. Any death—a wounded lioness separated from her cubs, a herd of stampeding elephants, marauding Wagogo—was preferable to this. As his fellow workers topped the verge of the embankment, great carts of rock and earth in hand, there was no question, no hesitation, as they dropped their loads and fled. I watched in horror as the man tried desperately to crawl up the embankment, away from the reptile's clutches, to get help, anything, only to be met with a wall of rock and mud careering down towards him. He and his captor were immediately buried in that embankment, forever, the mud sucking both snake and victim to their doom. There was no means of retrieving the body and he was left to slumber in his monumental tomb for eternity.

Although such accidents caused much consternation among the men there was nothing that could be done and the Germans would not tolerate any time-wasting on futile recrimination and discussion—a pointless exercise. The work had to go on.

It was drawing near to the great Muslim day of festivity, Ramadan, when we would slaughter many beasts, with much feasting, dancing and prayer to celebrate this great Islamic occasion.

Since there were so many followers of Islam among us the chief construction engineer was approached and, to our great delight, a public holiday was proclaimed for this, the holiest of holy days. Permission was granted and immediately preparations were put in place for a full-scale operation. Some went to neighbouring villages to purchase cattle, sheep and goats for slaughter, while others gathered great gourds of honey. As it was a day on which the teachings of the great Mohammed were to be commemorated the believers would not be permitted to drink alcohol. Wives and daughters collected the fruit of the tamarind tree, which when pulped and mixed with water and boiled, produced a very palatable non-alcoholic beverage. A few labourers were allowed to return to Tabora to buy cheap scent from the Arab traders for the women and girls who were to display the many phases of the life of Mohammed, through a variety of intricate dances. We practised at length the songs glorifying Mohammed and all was in readiness for the twenty-four-hour festival. Many of the heathens and Europeans, through both curiosity and courtesy, joined the merrymaking.

The engineer had granted permission for a specified area within the camp to be used. After clearing stumps and other obstructions, we erected simple tables and platforms made from brushwood.

The day of festivity dawned and during the hours of light we held constant prayers to the glorification of Mohammed. At dusk all the people, including the non-believers, were asked to bear witness to the great event that was to follow. The sheik of this community of Islam had said the final evening prayers and all were called upon

to watch, in silence, the dancing and singing about to take place.
As guests of honour the Europeans sat around the makeshift tables. They were the first to be offered the many varied drinks produced from the natural fruits of the land. Many of them had brought along their own alcoholic drinks, whether out of disrespect or mere ignorance of the significance of the occasion, we did not know. We prayed to Mohammed on their behalf to forgive them their ignorance and arrogance.

To open the ceremony the sheik chanted a long song to the glory of Mohammed. His voice, clear as a whistle yet swathed in mysticism and reverie, rose into the night. His assistants moved from person to person, spraying them with scent while wafting incense burned from swaying censors. The air hung thick with the heavy scents, filling our lungs as we breathed in deeply, filling our heads with their familiarity, as cups were filled with the sweet, cool nectar. When the sheik had finished, an announcer in full Islamic robes, called upon the first performers of the evening. A group of men approached the platform, carrying the flag of Islam. In pure, beautiful Arabic, they chanted songs, telling of the history of the great faith. The flag was placed in the middle of the stage and they circled it, starting to dance and sing. Their movements were vigorous and strong. The strength and passion with which they sang resonated in their booming voices and strong, muscular forms. Their dancing was so energetic that they soon began to glisten in the firelight, sweat saturating their bodies. Each movement was powerful and defined yet gentle in its execution.

The dance was halted by the sheik and in the European manner he proposed a toast to the great Mohammed and the faith of Islam. The dancing continued, growing more and more vigorous as time went on. Never once did they falter in movement or step but slowly their eyes began to glaze over and one by one they dropped to the floor with exhaustion. Their celebration and glorification of Islam had sapped them completely—yet they were fulfilled.

Huge bonfires were lit to throw more light on the gyrating, festive scene, as well as for cooking the enormous quantities of meat that had been prepared for the occasion.

The moon, which was in its first quarter, had just appeared over the trees, throwing its pale beams over the whole scene. At this exact moment the sheik called for silence and a complete cessation of all dancing. A prayer was offered to Mohammed. This was the sign to slaughter the beasts and bring the carcasses into the ring of celebration, to be cut up and given to all to cook on the great fires. For a while the entire gathering was preoccupied with satisfying its hunger.

Again the sheik uttered a command and the robed announcer introduced the first female performers.

These girls, ranging in age from eleven to fourteen, performed the dances of the concubines and slaves. Their dance was a sumptuous rolling of voluptuous hips in rhythm to the stamping of their feet. Each part of their bodies seemed to be participating in a different dance, yet they danced one dance—feet stamping, hips swaying and breasts shaking. Their high-pitched singing must have been heard for miles around. Some invisible signal parted the line of girls and the main feature, an older girl, appeared among them. She was tall and slim, her body lithe and perfectly proportioned as though carved by the hand of Mohammed himself. Her skin tone was a magnificent copper hue. She was naked, aside from a tiny thong between her thighs. Her stature was regal and sensuous and as she moved forward, pawing the ground with her feet, she started rolling her hips, slowly at first, then faster as she picked up the beat with her feet. Every part of her body vibrated in complete unison. She lolled her upper body sideways and backwards in circular movements, occasionally thrusting her body forward, and thereby introducing a new phase and form to her dance.

The effect of these gyrations was hypnotic and the Europeans, who had been conversing quietly, were instantly silent, watching in utter fascination this fluid body sliding toward them on the base of the drums and the thin notes of the reed pipes. In this mesmerizing manner she danced and, after some time, with the same grace as she'd made her entry, passed between the line of girls and disappeared from view.

Again the girls started singing and chanting, slowly moving away from the platform towards the spectators, their destination the Europeans who sat entranced. Closer and close they came, stamping their legs, swinging their arms and shaking their budding breasts. As they reached the table of guests they threw themselves erect, forming a single line. Then, leaning over backwards, they rolled as a wave, shuffling their way back to the platform, all the while singing in their shrill voices.

These were the first of many scenes to be performed throughout the night. Between each more eating and drinking took place and through the night men, boys and girls danced as the feast continued.

As the sun rose the events of the night drew to a close with numerous prayers and songs of praise to Allah, the great God.

XVII

After two long months the Malagaraise River crossing was complete. The rail line followed the foothills of the Buha highlands, snaking its way to Uvinza, which was to be a major station because of its valuable salt supply. A European company had further developed the salt-water spring. From the spring large quantities of salt were extracted and supplied to the townships along the line of rail, as well as to Dar es Salaam and Zanzibar. The salt was pumped out of the spring into great earthen pans where the water was evaporated by the sun, leaving behind a layer of pure salt, which was then packed into bags and transported by rail to each station.

From Uvinza station the line hugged the northern bank of the Malagaraise River towards Ujiji and Kigoma on the shores of Lake Tanganyika. Before reaching Kigoma, which had been selected as a site for a harbour, the river fanned out into a large delta with much swampland between the fingers of flowing water. In order to traverse the delta drainage channels were excavated by hand, diverting the main flow of the river from the embankment construction. Many thousands of tons of soil were extracted from the drained swamps and replaced with even greater quantities of rock and gravel, over which the railway line was to pass.

Progress was slow but inevitably we arrived at our final destination, Kigoma.

The work, however, did not stop at the end of the line and it seemed the development would never end. The next task facing both engineers and labourers alike was the construction of a major harbour at Kigoma—a harbour big enough for a large ship to dock. It was planned that this vessel would be used to facilitate trade up and down the shores of Lake Tanganyika.

To commemorate the completion of the railway line from Dar es Salaam to Kigoma the Kaiser son's, the Crown Prince, was set to arrive from Germany to hammer the final nail into the last sleeper. Some days passed while we awaited his arrival and we spent the time in a leisurely fashion, shooting and fishing.

At last the day arrived and, bedecked with flags, bunting and other decorations, the first official passenger train from Dar es Salaam steamed into Kigoma station. On the front of the engine was the German coat of arms, garlands of flowers and the German flag. All the *askaris* had been paraded and lined up on the station platform to await inspection by the Crown Prince. As he stepped from the train the chief engineer and commanding officer came to attention and bowed in greeting. He was taken on an inspection of the guard of honour and then a conducted tour of the station and the harbour, which was still under construction. After a thorough inspection of the area he returned to his coach on the train and we were dismissed. He would officially declare the railway line open to all traffic the following day and we were put on standby to await further instructions.

The following day was to be a public holiday and much drinking and celebration took place during the night. Day dawned and we were ordered to fall in on parade. After some drill we were marched along the railway line, in preparation for a final inspection by the Crown Prince, which would mark the end of the ceremonies.

At about ten o'clock the Kaiser's son, resplendent in a white uniform, trimmed in much gold and silver, and wearing a helmet bedecked with coloured plumes, arrived with the engineer, commanding officer and other construction staff. He again approached the parade and inspected the guard of honour, after which we were instructed to stand at ease. The prince addressed his audience and made a long speech on the benefits the railway line would bring to the country. He thanked everyone who had worked so hard and for so long on the project.

He then stepped forward and was given a hammer and a nail that was to be driven into the last sleeper at the end of the railway line. With great dignity he placed the nail in position and drove it, with just a few strokes of the hammer, into the sleeper. Immediately the air ignited with bugles blowing over the cheering of many thousands of voices.

He went on to tell us that in the near future the biggest boat that any of us had probably ever seen would be brought to Kigoma and launched on the lake. He added that it was made entirely of steel and iron. It burned firewood that produced steam to propel it. He left a few days later but we stayed on as a guard detail to keep watch over the construction site.

Many, many months passed and with the onset of 1913 came news of the pending arrival of the big boat in Dar es Salaam. The first sections of the ship, which would be known as the

Liemba, arrived a couple of months later. These sections were off-loaded at the water's edge where a special embankment had been built on which stood a battery of rollers. It was here that the Europeans started putting together the various parts. It was truly magnificent. Huge sheets were assembled and riveted to form the hull, which was in itself bigger than a house. Into the hull were placed the engines that would drive the ship through the water. There were no sails—it would be powered by great steam engines and driven by two propellers at the stern.

It took four months to complete the construction of the boat. The governor of German East Africa arrived to launch the *Liemba*. Again, as before, there was much parading and pageantry. Many locals gathered to watch, not fully believing that such a massive structure could actually float, let alone move. A bottle of champagne was broken over the ship's bow; wooden wedges were removed from the slipway and splash! The ship slipped easily into Lake Tanganyika and there, to the amazement of many, floated.

With the final fittings complete she was loaded with large quantities of firewood, and her engines were started and tested. The Europeans looked satisfied with everything and then, with flags flying and the ship bedecked with much bunting, the governor stepped aboard and the *Liemba* began her maiden voyage over the open waters of Lake Tanganyika. She was to follow the eastern coast of the lake down to the farthest, most southerly point. On the way she'd collect from the villagers dried fruit and other produce and advertise to all the splendour of German development. The ship would also take on board paying passengers.

Six days later she berthed at Kigoma. The ship was off-loaded, the passengers disembarked and the governor returned to Dar es Salaam.

At long last a great stage in the development of Tanganyika was complete.

How little any of us realized that so much of this great effort was to be shattered by war—a white man's war, the like of which the country had never experienced in all its history.

෯෯෯

The pale, shredded beams of golden light cast by the half-moon rising through the trees cast a mosaic of shadows across the dying embers of the campfire.

Mzee Ali awoke from his reveries.

We shivered in the cold night air and knew it was time to come away from the past and seek sleep in the last hours of the night.

PART III

XVIII

Many days of routine safari work passed before the opportunity arose when the leisures of camp life could once again be enjoyed. It was one evening as the screech of an owl was borne on the wind that Mzee, who had narrated nothing more of his life, sat up abruptly and embarked upon a further episode of his bygone days. In the year 1914, on just such a night, the *asakris* and Europeans of the German East African Army had been sitting around a campfire in a similar manner, talking of the day's work when he first heard of the outbreak of war.

Mzee sat staring into the fire, his face lit up occasionally by the flickering of the flames, his old mind stretching far back into the past. He began to recall how it was, that in the latter part of 1914, they had received news that a great and terrible war had broken out between Germany and other European nations. Transfixed by the flames he spoke, haltingly at first but the deeper he delved the clearer the memories became and the more easily his story flowed, immediately engaging us.

ক্ষ ক্ষ ক্ষ

From the talk around the campfires we knew this was to be no ordinary war. The sheer scale of it set it apart from any war we had known or been involved in. We heard news of developments on Germany's western and eastern fronts, campaigns taking place in faraway lands. We knew from the gravity of the discussions that this war would come to our land and that only then would we fully comprehend its nature.

All troops and men were ordered to assemble in Tabora. Our officers were to prepare us in full military readiness to fight the British and the Belgians. The training was intense. We were once again taught how to fight and how to defend ourselves, but in a new style of warfare. Many of us were seasoned by hardship but the new recruits found the training almost unbearable, as the idea of war seemed to pinch the already merciless attitudes of our officers. Even those of us who had previously served under them found the training gruelling.

In April 1915, we boarded a train to Morogoro. From there we were transported to Moshi, a small town near Mount Kilimanjaro. There we received further training. When we were deemed ready for combat we were moved to the front lines for our first meeting with the enemy.

Reports indicated that British and Indian troops had advanced south along the coast and captured the port of Tanga. This was very bad news for the Germans and indeed for us, but there was little time to dwell on it. The plan was for us to capture the railway line between Mombasa and Nairobi and between Voi and Taveta. At this stage we were stationed at El Oldoroba, an outpost near the main road to Taveta.

Two platoons, commanded by eight European officers of

varying ranks, were ordered to advance on a position within two miles of Taveta. I was in one of these platoons. Our advance was not hazardous as the bush was thick and the grass dense in that area, providing ample camouflage and we were thus able to move freely during daylight. At our predetermined destination we were assembled and underwent a thorough weapons and equipment check. Again we moved forward and, on nearing a hill called Salahita, were ordered to halt and take cover. Here we were to remain concealed for the rest of the day, to continue our advance under the cover of darkness.

It was difficult to rest. Although we had not as yet seen any combat we knew we were not far from it. The scale and horror of this war had magnified out of all proportion in our minds. My sweaty hands were slippery as I gripped my weapon, trying to find some solace in its feel. But instead of comfort my mind was hurled back many years, when the Germans had first conquered our land, to basic training—to that day in the blazing sun when we had fumbled and dropped our rifles. Exhaustion took over and I drifted into a half-sleep only to be plagued by these memories. I dreamed of an efficient, well-drilled enemy. I dreamed we were fumbling and struggling to handle our rifles. I dreamed I was under heavy fire and my weapon, as hard as I might try, was always just out of reach. I slowly surfaced from my half-sleep to find I was soaked through with sweat. Breathing deeply to control my nervousness I determined to put my faith and indeed my life in my training and in our officers.

My platoon consisted mostly of men with whom I had worked alongside for many years. There were a few new recruits but they seemed confident and capable. Our commanding officer was a man I respected and trusted. With this new resolve I was able to sleep more easily in the late afternoon sun.

When darkness fell we moved still closer to Taveta, which was by now only a short distance away. We travelled as soundlessly as possible, staying in constant contact with each other. This cautious approach, all the while crouched, putting one boot in front of the next in a deliberate manner, took several hours.

The moon was far into its second quarter when we were ordered to halt, sit down and wait. A scouting party of four Europeans continued to reconnoitre the area to our front. They suspected British troops were holding Salahita Hill. When they returned we were ordered to proceed cautiously to a concealed riverbed near the foot of the hill.

The attack on Salahita and Taveta would take place at dawn. It was our intention to obtain information regarding the enemy's disposition rather than actually capturing any ground.

With bayonets fixed and rifles loaded and cocked we waited in silence for the dawn.

With the fading of night day broke as it had a thousand times before, the darkness penetrated by a dim haze below the horizon, the sounds of night replaced by the waking of birds and animals. Yet this dawn would change us forever—this day would bring with it a baptism the likes of which we could never have imagined. Up to this point we had always had the advantage of fire-power. Whether fighting warring tribesmen or stampeding animals whose territory we'd invaded we'd always held the upper hand. Now we faced an enemy with equal, if not superior, fire-power. It was to be our first real battle and the first time our rifle-fire would be answered with rifle-fire, and worse, machine-gun fire—and the first time perhaps that our attack would be answered with their counter-attack

From a distance of some thousand yards a machine-gun opened fire in our direction from the British positions on the hill. The bullets passed over our heads but the intention was clear. It was not so much the loudness of the sound but rather the danger it carried with it. Behind us the ground shivered. We shivered. Our cover was thick and we advanced in spurts from thicket to thicket, making it difficult for the machine-gunners to find their mark. No one was hurt and the sound of firing settled easier on us. In our hearts the belief that we were in no particular danger had crept in and we continued our advance unscathed.

Suddenly all went quiet, the machine-gun had stopped firing— we thought the enemy must have retreated. We were now only a matter of some two hundred yards from the base of the hill, separated by an open clearing. It was not a natural clearing— the remnants of trees and bush were evident from the stumps protruding from the ground. It had been cleared by the enemy as a field of fire. From our position to the safety of cover at the foot of the hill, this stretch of open ground spanned some fifty yards— fifty yards in which we would be completely vulnerable and plainly visible. We were ordered to advance in twos and threes, so as to make it more difficult for the enemy to shoot us, and then re-group at the base of the hill, close to an outcrop of large rocks.

The commander, another European and five *askaris* made the first dash. Instantly the machine-gun on the hill sprang to life, emitting a volley of bullets trained directly on the charging men. They ran as though the devil himself were chasing them, but the odds against them were too high and directly a bullet ripped through one of the *askaris'* legs. He fell face forward, writhing in pain, drawing his legs in to his stomach and clinging to them, rocking back and forth. He was calling for help, but it would have been suicide for the men with him to stop or for one of us to go out there and get him. Five or six strides farther the commander reeled back as though he'd met with some invisible wall. He staggered, trying in vain to regain his balance, but another volley of bullets laid him in the dust, the sand darkening beneath him. Then another *askari* was hit, the bullets tearing his chest apart.

It was difficult to focus on the task ahead—we were next, but the wounded man in the clearing was still moaning, the pain stifling his voice yet his complaints still audible.

To live, to make it across, I would have to combine the essence of my training—that we were to work as a unit—with my natural instinct for survival. For the first time in our military experience we were now truly facing war—and death.

As I left the safety of my cover, running, doubled over, all sense of reality left me and I found my self being carried forward by some unknown force. I was aware of each individual passing moment as if the seconds had been separated from one another. Bullets were tearing up the ground in front of me and behind me, ripping through the body of the man in front of me. I leapt over his fallen form and bullets cracked through the air to my left and right. I felt I would be hit at any moment. Four of us made it across, but we knew that eight of our comrades lay dead or dying in the open ground behind us.

The officer who had remained under cover with the bulk of the platoon decided to break up the rest of the men into smaller sections. They would make the dash across at the same time but at different places, thus making it more difficult for the enemy to pick them off. In this way many *askaris* got through. We formed up in the lee of the rocks and, with a right flanking movement, swung up the slope towards the machine-gun emplacements.

Sixty yards from target the order was given to charge. It was a terrible thing. Bullets flew all about us, some killing, others wounding. Men lay on the ground crying out in agony, crying out for their mothers. Officers shouted orders, trying to make themselves heard above the din. The enemy trenches were now in sight and we could make out the enemy troops firing furiously at us.

Fortunately we were able to return fire from the relative safety of the bush and rocky outcrops on the hill. Once close enough, our officers threw grenades into the trenches and ordered us to immediately close with the enemy, bayonets fixed. Bayonet fighting is savage and it was here that we were to experience our first unpleasant taste thereof. Although your survival and the survival of the men in your platoon are always at the forefront of your mind, this type of combat is more personal, as now the enemy has a face, the fear and fire in his eyes reflecting yours.

The outpost was overrun and captured with comparative ease. To our surprise it had been held by only a small number of enemy troops. But we were not to stay. We moved forward another hundred yards so as to evade any enemy artillery that might be trained on us. Should the enemy counter-attack, the enemy would be taken by surprise in finding their trenches empty, thus giving us an added advantage in being able to counter any attack with a flanking movement from their rear.

When the battle eventually drew to a close some men were sent back to attend to the wounded and bury the dead. Two messengers were dispatched to inform our battalion commander that the position overlooking the town of Taveta had been taken. He was also advised that we would remain in our present position but would fall back in the event of a determined enemy attack.

Strangely, the British made no effort to regain their lost ground, which was puzzling. Surely the positions they had previously held, now claimed by us, were strategically vital to them? Otherwise, why had they bothered to entrench and set up machine-gun posts?

We dug in at our new position and settled down to await the commanding officer and the rest of the battalion. During the night the entire battalion was deployed into an offensive position half a mile from Taveta and preparations began for a dawn assault on the town.

In order to capture the town we had to break through the enemy's first line of defence on the perimeter, defended by entrenched infantrymen and machine-gun nests.

The town itself was small—it consisted of only a few stores, the railway station, several European houses of brick and mortar and a scattering of African huts set to one side.

If we had for one minute thought that the previous day's fighting had prepared us for the true horrors of war, we were sorely mistaken.

The town and surrounding bush erupted almost immediately. The ground shook with the barrage of artillery and mortar explosions. Enemy machine-gun fire raked our positions and already there were fatalities. Our officers bellowed out the order to charge and our step did not falter. From concealed positions we returned fire and commenced our systematic assault. Running, diving behind a fallen tree, a rock, then firing, re-loading, then running again, quickly finding safety behind an anthill, breathless, the cordite-filled air stinging our nostrils. A quick burst of fire from around the anthill and then running again. We were so focused that when the next salvo of explosions shook the earth we hardly noticed. Amidst the yelling and screaming I felt quite alone. The smoke was so thick that I couldn't see a single person and I could feel the panic rising, as in every other *askari*. Like bile, I fought desperately to suppress it, to keep it at bay, to listen for my commanding officer's voice above the mayhem, the harsh voice of comfort. But I could not distinguish one voice from another—the shellfire was so intense and hearing anything, besides the wailing of the dying, was almost impossible. Gradually my eyes became accustomed to the cloying smoke and the panic slowly subsided. Two of my comrades were at my side, only a couple of yards away. All we had to go on were our primary orders and we got to our feet, keeping low and, like machines, began once again to advance.

I was no longer running, the ground had opened up and the deafening explosion had sent me reeling backwards. I landed hard and struggled for breath. It came only in short, sharp, painful gasps. I looked about and saw one of the *askaris* splayed across the body of the other. He was dead and the man under him was screaming and pleading with me for help. I dragged myself over to where he lay and at first glance could find nothing wrong with him. I thought he was simply in shock and that the horror of his dead friend lying on top of him was too much for him to bear. When I finally managed to roll the corpse away I saw with horror the cause of his endless screaming. His legs had been blown clean off by the blast and blood was spurting out where his legs once were. There was nothing I could do but stare, transfixed by the appalling sight. His cries ebbed to a pitiful whimper as his life faded. It did not take long for him to die, his eyes staring in an awful grimace.

Slowly I became aware of the voice of my commanding officer urgently calling us to re-group on him and I pulled myself away. We were very close to the British trenches and it was time to bombard them with grenades and commence the bayonet charge. We re-positioned ourselves according to his instructions and waited for the signal. This time the screams and cries of anguish now came from the other side but there was no time for pity. No sooner had the grenades exploded than we were signalled to launch the final charge. And charge we did.

Firing and yelling as we ran, we reached the enemy positions and tumbled in a wave of fury into the trenches. Shocked and terrified British and Indian troops, in various stages of disarray, were there to meet us. Bayonets fixed we fought, no farther than a pace or two from the other. As I landed in the foot of the trench I rammed the sharp steel of my bayonet into the nearest victim. He had his back to me, attending to a wounded soldier lying against the rear wall of the trench. The impetus of his fall freed my bayonet to strike again and I turned to my right, narrowly missing the tip of an enemy bayonet. I used my rifle to swing him off balance by striking the butt against the side of his rifle. He lost his footing but, in the process of drawing back my rifle to strike again, he was on his feet in an instant, lunging forward. I sprang backward, stumbling over a slumped body and landed clumsily on my backside. There was no time to get up. The man was almost upon me, the tip of his bayonet now a foot away from my chest. I rolled desperately to the side as he lunged at me for the coup de grâce and, by the grace of God, he too fell clumsily over the form of corpse. Protruding from a holster still attached to the webbing of this unfortunate soldier was a revolver. He must have been an officer, but this thought only occurred to me much later. I ripped it from its keeping and, pressing it against the man's chest, fired. He slumped dead at my side—a brave and courageous man.

This gruelling hand-to-hand combat continued for what seemed an eternity. It was exhausting and horrific, it lost all sense of reality and I lost track of how many men I fought and killed. The conflict evolved into a hazy sea of frightened eyes, bloody flesh, mutilated corpses, screams, overlaid by gunfire distant and surreal, and an eerie wailing that was the very embodiment of hell.

Our force prevailed. We took the town and cut the main railway line from Mombasa to Nairobi.

We were instructed by the battalion commander to dig in and consolidate our position. Numerous patrols were sent out to establish where the retreating British troops had encamped.

Reports came back that their numbers were slim and that a counter-attack was unlikely.

It was here for the first time that General von Lettow inspected the battalion and warmly congratulated us on our achievement. More troops arrived and stronger defences were established to prevent the enemy from recapturing this strategic town.

Aside from a few minor skirmishes there seemed to be a general atmosphere of pause. We based up there until February 1916 when the South Africans attacked Salahita Hill. The fighting was fierce but the fortifications we had built held and they were unable to dislodge us. Their numbers were vast but during our bayonet charge they retreated—no, in fact, they ran—they turned and ran. These white men, this superior race, with their heavy artillery and overwhelming fire-power, turned and ran like rabbits.

It was then that we realized the cunning of the Germans—they had secretly brought up field artillery to repel any major enemy attack, however, when fired, these guns made such a noise that they frightened the *askaris* more than the enemy.

A month later we were attacked by a very strong force of South African, Indian, Rhodesian and British troops. In the March of 1916 we were forced to withdraw from Taveta to the hill at Salahita where we came under heavy artillery fire.

Realizing our predicament our commander, Major Kraut, sent word to General von Lettow that he was obliged to retreat towards the road that passed between the hills of Raeta and Latema. It was here that we consolidated our final position. General von Lettow was himself only five miles off at a place known as Himo. We were attacked many times. The enemy's numbers seemed to strengthen no matter how many casualties they took—yet ours continually diminished, forcing the general and our commanding officers to assume a more discerning strategy as to which battles we would fight and which we would not.

The enemy was determined to capture the road to Moshi. The ensuing battle lasted for many days where the advantage changed hands so many times that it was impossible to know when we were winning and when we were losing. Both sides suffered heavy losses.

With the fighting continuing unabated the enemy managed to flank our positions to the rear and, during that same month of March, they eventually launched their major assault and claimed the hill of Raeta. Major Kraut was more than aware that if we did not relinquish our current position we would be encircled and forced to surrender. General von Lettow therefore ordered a general withdrawal to Lahe. It was here that we learned of a second enemy army that had moved around the back of Kilimajaro and had captured Moshi.

It was now necessary for General von Lettow to take up a completely new position south of Moshi, on the Kahe–Ruwa line at the foot of the Pare mountains.

This was to be our operational base for some time to come.

XIX

We were being savagely attacked from both east and west by the South African and Rhodesian troops of General Smuts. As a result of this relentless pressure General von Lettow split his army into units of battalion-strength each. In this manner we moved in a southwesterly direction towards Mombo.

During the withdrawal we had to cross country inhabited by the Maasai tribe. We knew them as being belligerent and opposed to any form of civilized government. They had at one time been masters, not only of this land, but also of the Kikuyu country as far north as Mount Kenya.

The pressure of being continually chased by the South African and British forces never let up. It was during one of our many skirmishes that the platoon with which I was serving was cut off from the main force. Accordingly, we had to make our own way to a pre-arranged rendezvous point given by General von Lettow to his commanders. Our platoon commander immediately gave orders to cease firing, disengage and move back to a stream called Magiyangu.

We were in the process of withdrawing when the two lead scouts suddenly began shouting incoherently that danger lay ahead and turned tail and ran blindly into the bush. Their eyes had been keenly trained on the bush for any sign of enemy presence and had been so utterly startled by what they'd found that we were not able to fully comprehend the situation. They had forgotten where they were, that before this war the African bush held many dangers of its own. These dangers were still very real, but this was of little consequence as they ran, terrified, deeper and deeper into the bush. We froze in our tracks and as trained soldiers, dropped to one knee, facing out in all-round defence so as to cover any possible contingency. The bush was thick and matted, difficult to move in and see through. This had not, however, precluded the scouts from beating their hasty retreat. No sooner had they passed us by than a thundering stampede, seemingly a thousand-hoofs-strong, filled the air

At first we thought, as the scouts obviously had, that this was some sort of secret British weapon, but as soon as we saw the three bolting rhino, paying little heed to any obstruction in their path, we were forced to replace our military hats for our bush hats. Suddenly these animals were more dangerous than any European enemy and in haste we fired a volley of shots in their direction. We did not know whether they were hit or not.

Then something so bizarre happened that all we could do was stare in disbelief. Passing close to an *askari* a rhino had spotted him and with a great sweep of his head passed its horn between the *askari's* body and the leather belt he was wearing. Suspended on the end of the horn the enraged animal used the man's body as a battering ram to demolish any obstruction that came in its way. In this manner he was carried some eighty or ninety yards. The man, however, had not realized what had happened and was convinced he was the target of some new and brutal British weapon. Fortunately, his belt snapped, releasing him from his animal peg. He fell to the ground wailing and moaning, calling on Allah to protect him from this terrible monster. When we approached he still had his face buried in the ground, no doubt thinking the noise we were making was yet another onslaught. With his posterior protruding towards the sky in a most grotesque manner he screamed his praises to Allah all the louder. The platoon commander found it quite impossible to restrain himself and, further humiliating the unfortunate *askari*, placed a well-aimed boot on the man's backside with great force.

The result—a final cry to Allah for assistance—before fainting from shock. We poured some water over him, bringing him to his senses and it was only then that he realized what a fool he had made of himself. From that time on the *askari* would always be known by his new nickname 'Mtako'—backside.

Following this incident we gathered ourselves together and approached our rendezvous point on the Magiyangu River. We had no idea where the enemy was at this time and, as we followed the banks in a southerly direction, we hoped against hope that they had not yet infiltrated the area.

We had been marching solidly for forty-two hours and were exhausted. We were short of ammunition and food supplies and thus forced to avoid contact with the enemy at all costs. Towards evening, our platoon commander, aware of our fatigue and hunger, shot an eland bull. We ate well that night and dried the extra meat over our fires to take with us on the long journey south.

We rested for a day on the banks of the Magiyangu. Early the next morning we started again, hoping that on our southerly journey we would meet up with General von Lettow and the main force. For four days we kept going. Our meat supplies were running low and water was scarce. From time to time we met up with hostile Maasai tribesmen who tried to attack us with spears. We met their hostility with gunfire (warning shots, we had no quarrel with them) and they retreated and took cover. They would shadow us for some way before being completely satisfied that our intentions toward them were peaceful.

At last, on the fifth day, tired and hungry, we came upon von Lettow's army. We approached cautiously, breaking through some very dense elephant grass. We were so relieved at having found them that the shots fired at us from the perimeter of the camp came as such a shock that we were momentarily paralyzed. Had we mistaken an enemy encampment for our own men? Had the enemy overrun the camp? Our commander quickly assessed the situation—it was our straggling platoon that had been mistaken for the enemy. He broke cover and stepped forward confidently, shouting out that we were friend and not foe—only to be met with a volley of rapid fire that tore through him, cutting him down instantly. As one we ran to his aid, hoping there was still something that could be done, but we had all witnessed too much of war to know when a man could and could not be helped. He was dead by the time we reached him.

The perimeter guards, on recognizing our uniforms, realized their mistake. Their European officer came forward to investigate. He was dumbfounded by the unfortunate error and taking off his hat said a short prayer for his fallen comrade—a man who had brought us through many trials and difficulties, periods of hunger, thirst and situations requiring great courage and fortitude on his part. But war is war and regrettable mistakes are made.

When the commander had pulled himself together he instructed that the body of the dead officer should immediately be taken to command headquarters, fifty yards inside the perimeter. There his body was sewn into his groundsheet and buried under a large wild fig tree. His hat was placed on top of a cross, fashioned from local brushwood, and his name written in pencil on the hat. He was buried with full military honours as a true son of Germany. The loss of our commander—our mentor, comrade and friend— was deeply felt by the whole platoon.

After the burial we were assigned a new commander, who unfortunately did not prove to be of the same stature as our former officer.

We were constantly on the run, being squeezed between a vice. In an effort to crush us the British pushed hard along the main railway line stretching from Tanga to Moshi, but we managed to slip from their grasp, retreating farther south to Wilhelmstahl. Here General von Lettow spread out his forces in a semi-circle around the town, hoping to lure the enemy into a frontal attack and thereby to destroy him in a pincer movement. But the troops of General Smuts were no longer foreign to the country and had learned much since the original actions around Moshi. Instead of a frontal assault, they encircled our forces in the shape of a horseshoe, attempting to cut off our avenue of retreat. The general saw this clever move and ordered an immediate attack, hoping to fool the enemy into believing that he was committing superior forces into battle. In the meantime he put in place the lines of retreat in case the enemy were too strong and counter-attacked in force.

Although short of food, we had sufficient weaponry and ammunition. Early on the Wednesday morning we attacked, capturing considerable ground before the enemy realized what had happened. They immediately sent in reinforcements and in their counter-attack managed to reclaim the ground they had lost.

It was a fierce battle—with machine-guns, mortars and artillery wreaking their usual manner of havoc. I was positioned behind a mound of earth thrown up by a shellfire explosion. My intention was to fire a few rounds in the direction of a persistent machine-gun nest and then advance to a low wall near their position. I had just risen to dash across the short distance when a bullet tore into my leg, a little way below the knee. My first thought was not terror, but dismay—I could not believe that the war was over for me.

The pain was bearable, more a foreign sensation, but I was not able to walk and it was only later, after being examined by a doctor that I understood my predicament. My friends refused to leave me to be captured by the British and carried me all the way to our rear-base position at Wilhelmstahl.

From there I was put on a mule train to Mombo where I was admitted to hospital. I was well cared for by doctors and nurses. The pain increased daily but there was little the doctors could do for me as they were fast running out of medicines. They were obliged to resort to using local herbal medicines provided by nature. My leg had swollen considerably and was starting to smell.

The doctor allowed the huge blue flies to rest on the wound and lay their eggs in it. In a short space of time these hatched into maggots that ate away the rotting flesh. The maggots did their job well and it was only after this that the doctor dressed the wound with fresh cow dung obtained from a nearby kraal.

As the wounded poured into the little hospital so news of the war reached us. Our troops had been forced to retreat farther south to the main telegraph station at Mombo and then again to Hundeni, a main hospital depot, even farther south. At Hundeni my leg healed and after a short rest I was sent to rejoin the front-line forces.

We had been at Hundeni some two months when General von Lettow marched into the town and told us that both Wilhelmstahl and Mombo had fallen and that from here on he was going to conduct the war along the style of the Boer commandos, who had recently fought the British during the South African War, and that, in this manner he would never be captured.

Three days later we moved in a westerly direction towards Mtazi, crossing the Mjongo River and then northeast to Kondoa-Irangi. All the while the enemy where hot on our trail and there was little time to rest. Our forces were being rapidly depleted, not only as a result of the fighting but also from the incessant scourge of malaria and other illnesses. Thus, whenever we reached a village, all men and boys over the age of sixteen were immediately conscripted into service as porters or *askaris*. Their basic training was brief but drastic measures were needed to overcome the problem of manpower shortages.

The new recruits were generally in awe of us, veteran fighters that we were, and thus we were frequently able to make use of them as servants. We warned them that if they did not do our bidding they would be treated as slaves. On arrival at a town or village General von Lettow would commandeer food and livestock without any compensation to the owners. Village headmen were forced to supply sleeping quarters for the troops as well as young girls, thereby ensuring a good night's sleep and rested, satisfied troops.

From Kondo-Irangi we travelled across the southeastern extremity of the Serengeti plains, heading for Dodoma. In this barren country there was plenty of game, but water was extremely scarce. The general had recently blazed a trail with the main army across the plains to Dodoma. He had dispersed smaller units in a fan around the general line of withdrawal to prevent any enemy pincer movements or attempts to cut off his retreat. Communications were bad, with our commander knowing only the general direction of Dodoma.

We came across a few tribesmen on the way but they had clearly been terrorized by German rule and were disinterested in passing on any information regarding the position of the enemy or of the railway line—or of Dodoma for that matter. Having left the last 'civilized' village behind we began encountering the difficulties and problems experienced by any trekker in this part of Africa. Water was scarce, maps inadequate and all our officer could do was guide us on a compass bearing, hoping that we would reach the railway line on one side of Dodoma or the other. We shot some game for food but by nightfall it had been twenty miles since we'd left the last village and the possibility of finding water before reaching Dodoma was slim. Some of the troops did not understand the severity of the problem or the harshness of the country in which they found themselves and foolishly squandered their meagre water supplies on cooking and drinking, leaving nothing for the morrow.

At dawn the next day we fell in and marched in ragged formation in a southwesterly direction. The sun rose higher and higher in the sky and with its ascent the heat increased. There was no water in sight. Midday came and still no sign of water—even the game was beginning to diminish, a worrying indication that this region held precious little water. The constant marching on this dry, barren plain, raised clouds of dust, further aggravating our intolerable thirst. Our black faces had taken on a brick colour and the faces of the Europeans were red and blistered from sunburn. The commanding officer warned us that only with his express permission were we to take a single sip of what water remained in our canteens. As the sun moved westward so our parched throats worsened, making even the act of swallowing difficult. Not only were we desperately dehydrated we developed agonizing cramps as we marched. Those who could not keep up were disarmed and left behind, either to die or catch up in their own time. Trees and bush were scarce so there was little shade where these poor souls could seek refuge.

As night fell we were allowed one cup of water each and were forced to chew half-raw calf meat as our evening meal. We sprinkled a little salt on the meat to aid our dehydrated bodies. But in solving one problem we only aggravated another, our insatiable thirst. We would bivouac in this barren area for a short while and were instructed by our commander to take as much rest as possible in the time allotted.

At around midnight we were awakened by the sound of sporadic firing in the far distance to the east. We were ordered to stand-to immediately and waited anxiously, wondering whether it was enemy fire or troops like us, lost in this unforgiving country.

After a short while the commander again ordered a general withdrawal in the direction of a compass bearing he had taken on Dodoma. About an hour later we saw flashes of gunfire and heard small-arms fire some two miles off. We were ordered to dig foxholes and form whatever hurried fortifications we could in preparation for an enemy attack. Four scouts were sent out in the direction of the gunshots to carefully observe the source of the gunfire and report back as soon as possible. Before they left the firing started up again, this time closer to our position than before. These were anxious moments—no one knew what lay ahead, what the war had in store for us on such a night. New instructions were issued to the patrol—once they had established who was firing they were to fire one red flare into the air if it were enemy fire and then retreat in our direction as quickly as possible. We would fire one shot to indicate our position. However, should it turn out that they were in fact a lost unit, such as ourselves, they were to fire two green flares, to which we would reply with one green flare.

The patrol moved off, leaving us entrenched and in great suspense.

It must have been some three hours later when we heard an exchange of fire about one and a half miles distant. We immediately saw one red flare shoot up into the sky, followed immediately by more rifle-fire. Then seconds later two green flares were fired, causing much confusion for our commander. Had our patrol managed to capture some enemy troops, in which case who had the enemy initially been fighting? Or was it a patrol like ours? There was but one thing to do—wait and see.

Towards dawn we could make out distant silhouettes on the skyline. We were tense, the tension exacerbated by our fatigue. We traced the outlines of the figures with the muzzles of our rifles, with orders to hold fire until the commander could establish with some degree of certainty whether the forms were friend or foe. Even through his night binoculars he was having difficulty distinguishing the uniforms.

Two more men were sent forward, crawling on their hands and knees, with instructions that if the figures on the horizon were enemy they were to open fire. This would give the commander a chance to organize us into some sort of attack formation. Minutes passed like hours as we watched the two snake forward on their bellies, heads down, occasionally daring to sneak a glimpse ahead.

Suddenly they stood up and we all breathed a deep sigh of relief. Our anxieties were done with, for what we'd feared to be enemy forces were in fact friends, suffering in the same way as ourselves.

It transpired that they were without food or water, having consumed all they had the previous day. Moreover, they were completely lost and had been firing shots in the air in the hope of attracting attention—regardless of any enemy presence. It was their good fortune that we were in the area and had heard their shots. Our commander ordered a small quantity of water to be dispensed to each of the twenty *askaris* and the one non-commissioned officer. This European was badly burned and suffering from heat exposure. There was to be no rest for either him or his men—or for us for that matter, for in this treeless waste there was nowhere to shelter from the burning rays of the merciless sun.

Our commander, now the officer in charge of both units, ordered the troops to prepare themselves for the day's march. We fell in and trudged off, plodding along wearily with the tiniest flicker of hope in our hearts that our destination was not too far away. The blistering day slowly passed and night eventually came. Too weary to lay down our blankets or any other form of meager comfort, we collapsed to the ground and lay where we fell, caring naught for wild animals, snakes or any other pest found in that dreadful terrain. Occasionally the odd scream was heard, breaking the silence of the night—most likely a restless sleeper rolling onto a scorpion. The night was a living hell and only a few of us succeeded in getting the sleep we so desperately craved. Not only did we endure scorpion stings and snakebites but also the relentless heat that barely abated during the night. In the case of scorpion stings, the wounds were simply cut open and left to bleed, but with snakebites there was little that could be done, apart from cauterizing the bite with burning embers from the night's fire in an effort to halt the spread of the poison. Four men died that night as a result of snakebites.

At one o'clock in the morning the commander ordered us to fall in. He had decided that we should march as far and as fast as we could during the hours of darkness, being marginally cooler than daylight. We would take what shelter we could find during the heat of the day.

And so we pressed on until dawn when we were told to find ourselves what shelter we could in the nearby scrub. We managed to sleep until mid-morning when the heat and swarming flies made rest quite impossible. Some comfort was taken in the fact we were not marching—we could not sleep but at least we could rest.

At sundown we were allowed a couple of sips of water each, our third drink in as many days, and instructed to eat half our partially dried meat. By moonrise we were again on the march. No one knew our exact position, the commander leading the way with his compass bearing. Estimating the mileage we had covered in the past four days we were sure the railway line could not be too far off, either that or we must surely be approaching Dodoma. We were staggering more than marching and cared little for the wild animals we came across from time to time. We did, however, take note that the game was more plentiful than it had been of late, meaning there had to be water somewhere nearby.

Some of the *askaris* were beginning to collapse and the stronger ones would shoulder their equipment and assist them. Although an added burden for us it kept together the waning spirit of the force. These were good, strong men whose bodies were failing them only because of the dire circumstances. We would not leave them behind—they were still an integral part of our proud unit.

At dawn the commander called a halt, listening intently in a particular direction. Sure enough we heard a rooster crow in the distance, faint but clear. Somewhere ahead of us lay a village …

and water … blessed water. We advanced cautiously, the promise of water driving us onward. We did not know whether our reception would be welcoming or hostile and scouts were sent forward to investigate. Just as the sun cut the horizon the scouts returned with news that we were only three miles from Dodoma and that a native village lay a short way ahead, tucked away in some dead ground to our front.

With joy and thanks to Allah for leading us out of the wilderness we pressed on. On entering the village the headman was called on by our commanding officer to produce food and water for the troops. His orders were duly obeyed and we slaked our thirst and ate our fill for the first time in five days.

As Dodoma was so close the commander decided we should stay at the village only long enough to eat and drink before moving on. We fell in, tired but restored, and with a guide from the village we marched on to Dodoma in rags and tatters, footsore and weary—but full of spirit.

What a sight we must have been. General von Lettow had arrived just a few days before and on our arrival congratulated us fiercely on the role we had played. We learned that the British were moving on Dar es Salaam and threatening our supply lines from the coast. British and Belgian troops had advanced on Tabora and were preparing for a major assault.

News from the front was grim.

However, General von Lettow agreed to allow us two days' rest, during which time we were to be re-equipped with new uniforms and ammunition.

The plan then was to move south again, this time to Iringa, and attempt to smash any enemy forces crossing the Dar es Salaam–Dodoma railway line.

Our ambition was great but we were confident in our leader and felt assured of success.

XX

After re-equipping the battalion was divided into two—one half to go by train to Kilosa and the other half, of which I was a member, to trek overland to Iringa through the bush.

We set off, our first stop at the village of Mloa, a day and a half out. It was an easy march as a road had been built—and more importantly, without incident. We waited two days for the arrival of our supplies before continuing with the next leg of our journey, which was to be a tough trek through unmapped forest country, for the most part unpopulated.

When all was in readiness we left Mloa with our scouts up front, blazing a trail through the bush. We covered some seventeen miles that first day. It was without incident, yet the tsetse flies were worse than ever and, as mules were liable to be stricken with sleeping sickness, it became necessary for us to travel only at night. The scouts continued during the day, felling trees and scoring others so that we could easily follow the trail at night.

Five days out from Dodoma we met up with a tributary of the great Ruaha River, which we followed. Firstly, because it was the only source of water in the area of which we were aware—and secondly, by following it we would eventually arrive at the Ruaha River itself. The going was tough, and although there was plenty of game to eat, lions, jackal and other wild animals molested us. We pressed on urgently, stopping as little as possible, since our instructions were to arrive at Iringa, re-equip and then move east to join up with another force coming from Utete, a small settlement on the banks of the Rufiji River.

Our orders were then countermanded, for when we got to Molasso on the Ruaha River we received revised instructions. We were to proceed immediately in the direction of Kisaki by following the river downstream. Intelligence reports indicated that a British force was closing in on Kilosa and Morogoro, and this, if allowed, would cut General von Lettow's forces in two. We understood the necessity of preventing this at all costs and so, with our meagre supplies, moved eastward, following the river.

The country was wild, heavily forested and ridden with tsetse fly, mosquitoes and other pests from which there was no escape. For four days we struggled through this terrible, uninhabited country, arriving eventually at another major tributary of the Ruaha. Our problem was then, how to cross this formidable river.

The rains were not far distant and already rain-laden clouds had started to build up, making it obvious that the first thunderstorms were imminent. We were not equipped for this sort of weather, the men were weary and we'd eaten nothing but meat. A lucky few had managed to find wild spinach with which to supplement their diet.

We camped on the banks of the river that night while the commanding officer deliberated as to the best method of crossing. He eventually decided that a large number of rafts should be built from logs bound together with rawhide strips. The rafts would be heavy, cumbersome and unsteady, but they would do the job and time was not a luxury we possessed.

The rafts were built and, anchored on the banks, proved easy enough to load with a fair amount of equipment and some twenty men apiece. We cut punting poles to propel the rafts through the river's current. There appeared to be little apparent danger.

Finally the rafts were ready and we pushed them off into mid-stream. The first raft was unsteady and the men were instructed to keep very still. Alas, fear is often stronger than common sense. Had the men obeyed their orders without question, in all probability they would have made a safe crossing, but unfortunately this was not the case.

The raft dipped slightly to one side and the two *askaris* closest to the edge spotted the long menacing shape hovering under the water, a few inches from their feet. To escape the crocodile they decided to change position, to a spot that appeared to be a little higher out of the water. As they rose to move the equipment started to slide, and with it slipped the wavering nerve of the other *askaris*, who immediately began to panic. Fright gripped them as they saw the water level rising on the one side of the raft. They too decided to move, thinking that by doing so they'd even the keel. This was a mistake. They misjudged the weight burdening the other side and the raft see-sawed, tipping steeply, resulting in a considerable amount of baggage sliding headlong into the river. And slide headlong it did, with men and equipment tossed clear of the raft into the swirling waters of the river. Even if they could swim, they stood little chance. The men were heavily laden with equipment, which dragged them down, the current pulling them under. The baggage sank immediately and the raft, now free of its load, righted itself and popped up like a cork. The side, which had previously been suspended in mid-air, came crashing down onto the heads of the men who were desperately scrambling to grab hold of the side.

The crocodiles were not slow in responding to this unexpected bounty. The first we knew of the hideous attack that followed was when we saw an *askari*, who had managed to struggle free of his equipment and was swimming towards the opposite shore, disappear with a scream and a flurry of water. Blood rose to the surface, turning the river red where the man had been drawn under, never to be seen again.

The commanding officer ordered us to fire a volley of bullets into the water in the vain hope of preventing a further attack. But before the order could be carried out two more men disappeared.

Pandemonium reigned both in the water and on shore. We vainly fired more volleys into the water as crocodiles surfaced. Two men were seen to reach the opposite shore while a further six, including a European, reached the reeds on our bank. The toll had been heavy. Apart from those killed by the bounding raft, crocodiles had taken three and the rest had drowned. All our equipment had been swept away.

The commanding officer issued orders to increase the size of the rafts still under construction—only a small area in the centre of the raft would be used for carrying purposes, with the remaining area kept free solely for buoyancy. As an additional precaution numerous rawhide thongs were plaited together to make a strong rope, which was to be tied to the raft from the shore so that in the event of another accident the raft could at least be salvaged.

For four days we laboured in the baking sun—building rafts, ferrying across goods and men, then returning to collect another load—and all the while the crocodiles lurked. Eventually all the remaining men and equipment were safely ferried across. Vigilant watch had to be kept up at night on both sides of the river. We worked non-stop in our efforts to conquer the mighty river and we succeeded but, as always, at no little cost. We were completely exhausted by the end of the fourth day, yet there was to be no rest. We were urgently needed on the battlefield, regardless of the strain and fatigue that overwhelmed us, not to mention those battling with fever and the constant stomach troubles caused by our sole diet of meat. Many were also suffering from infected wounds—some so septic that those afflicted suffered severe bouts of delirium.

The trek to Kisaki was set to commence.

No one knew what type of country lay ahead or whether there were any inhabitants in the area between the river and Kisaki. We hastily filled our water bags and canteens and dried meat over the fires.

The march resumed.

For several days bush, reeds, thick elephant grass, thorn trees and dangerous animals were our constant companions. For many days we marched with double loads, since some of the men were too sick to carry anything and themselves had to be carried on litters, further stretching our resources. When night arrived we settled in whatever available open space we could find. Strict instructions were issued regarding fires and the dangers of starting a grass fire out of carelessness. A fire, out of control, would destroy all our ammunition and equipment. Sentries were always posted to ward off undesirable visitors but still we hardly ever enjoyed a full night's sleep.

On one such night, utter exhaustion having fallen upon each and every man, a warning sounded by the sentry rudely reminded us that sleep was indeed a rare luxury. However, this alert was legitimate. Sweeping from the south, with a heavy wind behind it, came a major bush fire. Its flames licked at tree tops some twenty or thirty feet high. We worked feverishly with *pangas* to cut a fifteen-foot firebreak around the camp. But the wind driving the beast was furious and before long it was upon us, our firebreak a frail semi-circle around the camp. Men were diverted from the task of cutting the break to move the supplies to safer keeping. It all happened so fast. The sentry had called out the warning when it was a mere blur on the horizon. There were many hands working on that firebreak and yet, before we could complete the task, the fire was engulfing us—in a matter of minutes. Like spears, the strong wind threw blades of burning grass ahead of its path—in this way the fire seemed to leap-frog ahead of itself, consuming itself as it spread. This effect brought in our first casualties, encircling and trapping men in the flames. Some managed to cut a firebreak around themselves, but others were literally consumed within seconds by the hungry flames and their screams and wailing filled the night. Some men, panicking, tried to make a dash through the inferno to the relative safety of the camp. They suffered severely, with flesh charred and dripping from their limbs in places.

Not only were we trying to escape death but so too were many of the animals in the surrounding bush. The men were being ravaged by flames, snakes, scorpions and even centipedes. It was chaos, and only through our help, from the seasoned men of Africa, that some semblance of order was restored.

Indeed, there is nothing more frightening than witnessing by the light of the flames, cobras and other snakes moving towards you at great speed with their upper bodies raised. The only thing to do is stand perfectly still. Their fear has primed them to strike at any obstacle in their path, thus you should not present yourself as one. But many of the porters lacked the courage to keep still as a six-foot cobra hurtled towards them, a foot of its body in the air, its hood fanning out on either side. And they just kept coming, dozens of them, pouring out of the grass. The slightest movement meant an instant bite and in some cases almost instant death. We had no snakebite serum with us—the only thing we could do was to cut away the flesh where the bite had occurred. The blood would pour out and hopefully the poison with it, but this was only successful in a few cases.

At last, dawn broke and with it the night of terror was gone. Like the fire that had passed on without respite so too we found ourselves preparing again to march. Broken and worn we fell in and continued on our journey to Kisaki.

The casualties who could not keep up the pace were ordered to proceed towards the town at their own speed. They carried with them as much equipment and supplies as they could, for there were not enough of us to carry everything.

That day was a living hell and stands out in my mind as one of the most gruelling of the war. We were gravely tired and the heat of the sun was murderous.

The country gradually grew more and more hilly and at long last, after staggering to the top of a hill, we were able to see trails of smoke rising from a village in the distance. Here we hoped to meet the main force. This was Kisaki. We learned that the British forces, in considerable strength, were less than two days' march away.

On arrival we were issued new arms, equipment and ammunition—but no rest. We were dispatched to the northern extremities of the town to take up battle positions. It was here, exhausted but battle-ready, that we were finally able to rest.

XXI

Dawn was breaking when we heard the thundering clap of an explosion to our rear. Bugles sounded stand-to. Men rushed to defensive positions, lugging their ammunition with them. It was a dawn attack—by the enemy!

We had no idea of the extent of their manpower, but we did know we were about to face a determined onslaught by the enemy in an attempt to capture the village of Kisaki.

We'd been slumped in our trenches, some men trying in vain to get some sleep, others relating the most imaginative accounts of our recent journey—however, it had been so eventful that it did not need much embellishment. This was our state when the bugle had sounded and with it, almost immediately, field artillery shells exploded some five hundred yards behind us. The enemy strategy was to cut off our lines of supply and cause general chaos in the rear. Which it succeeded magnificently in doing. Ammunition dumps where blown up, and the men who whose job it was to distribute the ammunition lay splayed on the ground. Mules and cattle were stampeding in their kraals, red-eyed and frothing at the mouth. They managed through pure hysteria to break out and bolted wildly, this way and that, too terrified to identify any avenue of escape.

We, on the front line, had not as yet been touched. All we could see were the flashes from the guns firing in our direction from emplacements on a ridge of hills some two miles away. We knew that somewhere between those guns and our positions was an advancing mass of enemy infantry.

This barrage to our rear, disrupting our communications and lines of supply, was a recent strategy of war and had taken us completely by surprise. The fear and anxiety that had risen so sourly in my belly that first day, advancing on the hill of Salahita, bubbled back. I could taste the bile at the back of my throat. I thought I was prepared, mentally, for this battle. I felt it could be no more intense than anything we had experienced thus far. At least I knew what to expect—or so I thought. This new enemy tactic was so sudden and so unexpected that my mind was thrown into a jumble of confusion. We had always been taught and had seen in practice that the first bombardment was to destroy the front lines of defence. I had no idea what would happen next and this was more frightening than the thought of battle itself.

The German artillery opened up in reply by firing their field guns in the direction of the flashes on the ridge. In some cases they scored direct hits, for we could make out in the distance the gun emplacements being blown apart, with dust, rocks and men flying in all directions.

From our position we could hear only muffled explosions, not the cries of the victims. But we saw their plight and it gave the whole scene a surreal complexion—but death it was nevertheless.

It was then that enemy artillery, well concealed in the dead ground not far from the front lines, opened up and, without warning, shells came screaming down upon us, exploding right in our midst, tearing our trenches to pieces. The barrage threw up a screen of smoke, dust, rocks and stones, which in turn became lethal missiles. Many were killed and many more wounded yet we had still seen no sign of the advancing enemy infantry. This above all else was so unsettling that—amidst the blood and severed limbs, the wailing and agony to which one never grows accustomed—panic whipped through the ranks.

We did not have to wait long—like ghosts they appeared through the gloom and pall of smoke. In the ever-increasing morning light and as the smoke began to clear, those of us who were still capable, fired as rapidly as we could at these spectres of doom. Our fire did not halt their advance as they dodged from bush to tree and back to bush, taking cover where they could and rapidly returning fire.

The sun burst over the horizon and with its first rays we saw the flashes of bayonets. With the element of surprise the enemy had suffered few casualties and were now only a hundred yards or so from our forward positions. We were firing constantly but to no avail. Suddenly a tide of bodies arose, seemingly from the earth itself, an unstoppable mass of screaming soldiers, charging towards us. Firing from the hip and with bayonets thrusting, they poured into our trenches.

This was no longer a tactical battle, no longer a defensive engagement to protect strategic territory—we were fighting for our lives, every man for himself, saving ourselves from slaughter. We desperately tried to hold them off but our commander had been killed in one of the first shell explosions to hit the trenches, causing general disorder and uncertainty among the men.

As a result of the bombardment to our rear we had no idea as to the position of our headquarters, let alone whether they still functioned. All we could do was to try and stay alive and maintain some semblance of contact with one another.

The human wave engulfed our positions and we fled.

We retreated to the south where we were joined by a number of other men, wounded stragglers and survivors, before withdrawing a further ten miles south. Here we met up with more Germans.

In the meantime the British had captured Kisaki and had advanced a further five miles before calling a halt to re-group and consolidate. A counter-attack was out of the question. The enormous loss of life and even larger number of wounded, in addition to the loss of equipment and ammunition, had yet to be fully assessed. The *askaris* were assigned to hastily made-up platoons under new commanders. We were quickly re-formed into a new fighting force and in this manner made an orderly withdrawal some several miles south to the village of Beho-Beho. Here we consolidated our position on a line of hills overlooking a sweeping valley with an imposing escarpment to the north. We dug in, presenting a formidable defence. We waited like this for two days, re-equipped with fresh arms and ammunition, fed and watered, and ready to face any oncoming attack.

It wasn't long before the enemy made an appearance on top of the escarpment to our front.

They attacked on the third day, but not at dawn as we had expected. Just before the sun had climbed to its highest point their field guns opened up, smashing into our front lines. More lives were laid waste in the dust of our fortifications, with burst sand bags burying them in shallow graves. We did our best to retaliate with the artillery and rifle power we had available but we were grossly outnumbered and outclassed. We watched the enemy infantry fan out across the valley like the shadow of the late afternoon sun. En masse they came forward, inexorably seeping closer and closer like the blood of our fallen comrades discolouring the earth. We poured all our available machine-gun and rifle fire into the mass but could not halt the attack.

We were in a good position—one that was not easy to overrun and we beat off their first assault. They re-formed and by nightfall were dug in a mere twenty yards or so from our front lines. We were in no position to counter-attack. We were severely short of both men and ammunition. And so we waited, through the longest night of my life. Awake, alert, my heart pounding, yet deathly tired. They would charge if we withdrew and attack if we did not.

They succeeded in driving us out of our trenches the following morning and again we found ourselves retreating, making for the Rufiji River crossing and the hinterland. Here we learned of the deaths of Selous, the great white hunter, and many South Africans and Rhodesians, at the hands of the Germans. This was a huge victory for us, for Selous' reputation was legendary. But we continued our retreat, moving south, always south, with the enemy in hot pursuit.

We learned of a battle at the coast, near the mouth of the Rufiji, where General von Lettow had made a brave stand with the remainder of his troops. He had been beaten and was moving south towards the Portuguese border. We had lost control of the entire length of the Rufiji— captured by the enemy—and with it a major German supply line. A German battleship had been sunk in the mouth of the river and with it valuable and desperately needed supplies.

But General von Lettow would not surrender and sent out small skirmish parties to harass groups of British forces. In doing so we were able to capture much-needed arms, ammunition and food. These supplies were transported to the army that was rapidly making its way towards the territory of Portuguese East Africa, also known as Moçambique.

In November 1917, we reached the Ruvuma River, the border between Tanganyika and Moçambique. In the meantime another enemy army had advanced into Tanganyika from the south via the Northern Rhodesian and Nyasaland borders [now Zambia and Malawi respectively]. Sweeping upwards in an easterly direction they met up with the British forces advancing from the north.

The only option left to us was to engage in guerrilla warfare. As the general paid no heed to borders he crossed into Moçambique to pillage the local villages for food supplies.

We crossed the Ruvuma River at a place called Mgomano, penetrating deep into Moçambican territory. The country was harsh, hostile and sparsely populated. Again, game became our staple diet, supplemented only with what grain we could plunder from the villages. In this manner we moved farther and farther south until General von Lettow decided to cut westward towards Lake Nyasa.

We rested on the shores of the lake and by plundering the lakeside stores and villages were able to replace our tattered clothing and find suitable material to attend to the wounded. It was not long before word reached us that we were again in danger and would have to move.

The general led us back into Tanganyikan territory through the Songeya district. Although always on the run we never missed an opportunity to have a crack at the enemy in hit-and-run skirmishes. By such means we were able to keep ourselves relatively well supplied with British arms and ammunition.

At Lungenberg, a place on the northern point of Lake Nyasa, we crossed into Northern Rhodesia. Never daring to travel by road we snaked our way west through thick, wild country. On and on we marched, pillaging as we went.

We were in tatters again, without boots and exhausted—but still General von Lettow would not surrender. He believed with all certainty that the Imperial German Army could not be defeated. We crossed the Abercorn–Kasama road and continued on to Lake Mweru. Here we managed a short reprieve and it appeared the enemy had lost track of us for the time being.

XXII

The time again came when General von Lettow decided to make a stand against the British. We had left German Tanganyika and were now firmly ensconced in British territory. Again, we were well supplied with food and clothing, taken without compensation from the locals.

We marched in an eastward direction. The plan was to make for Luwingu village, but before reaching the village would swing north towards the town of Kasama. Villagers had been forewarned not to thwart us in any way and thus we had no problem fulfilling our food requirements. We proceeded in this direction for ten days until we reached Chilibula Mission. Here we were ordered to halt and a scouting party was sent out to investigate the strength of the British position at Kasama. It was two days before our scouts returned with the news that it appeared the British were aware of our advance and were in the process of evacuating the town. This was joyous news for the general who immediately set about planning an attack to capture Kasama.

The plan was to divide our forces into three. One battalion would make a full frontal attack on the town, the second would encircle the southern perimeter via an escarpment and the third would advance on the town from the north across flat scrub country. As the third battalion was making ready they encountered some locals who, on seeing them, fled into the town screaming—alerting the British of our attack before we were all in position.

General von Lettow ordered an immediate frontal attack by the central battalion and gave the order to advance. As we neared the town we came under small-arms fire from soldiers hidden behind small outcrops of rock. Our artillery was ordered to fire a barrage of shells into the town itself. The boot of chaos and disorder was now on the other foot as residents and troops alike fled for cover, with the enemy panicking that their escape routes would be severed.

I was with the central battalion and when the first shells hit we immediately arranged ourselves into a flanking movement against the enemy who were holding up our advance from their rocky defences. The bush was dense, and although we could close with comparative safety, our speed of advance was greatly reduced.

Meanwhile, our forces closing in from the south had entered the township of Kasama near the gaol and had managed to dispose of what little opposition their was with little cost to themselves.

Our hostile intentions were quite plain to the enemy troops to our front. They deserted their rocky outposts and began retreating headlong through the bush towards the town.

By this time the northern battalion had taken control of the Abercorn–Kasama road and was advancing along this axis towards the town centre. Intermittent firing from their positions could clearly be heard. The troop advance from the north momentarily distracted the enemy, giving us the chance we'd been waiting for and we charged—bayonets fixed.

Capturing Kasama was comparatively easy. The enemy were outnumbered and outmatched and a useful amount of equipment and ammunition was captured. General von Lettow ordered the destruction, by fire, of the *boma*, the gaol and various shops and buildings in the town, but not before we were able to re-equip with clothing, boots and other necessities. The British *askari* prisoners we had captured were stripped of all their belongings and uniforms and told that, provided they did not go south, they could return to their villages.

We were not certain of the general's intentions. Our position in and around Kasama was consolidated and the immediate vicinity appeared to have been deserted by the enemy. However, we still had to exercise extreme caution, in case of snipers or other enemy agents lurking nearby.

We were ordered to move south along the Chambesi River–Kasama road, keeping to the bush so as not to be observed. As we progressed we came across numerous deserted villages, indicating that news of our advance had preceded us. The locals had no doubt fled to seek refuge with any British forces that lay ahead. With even greater caution we pressed on towards the Chambesi River where we knew there to be a British force dug in. Chambesi was strategically important as it boasted a rubber factory and a war-matériel depot that supplied the British military in the Abercorn and Old Fife districts.

It was November 1918 and it had been a while since we had heard any news from the European fronts.

About fifteen miles from Chambesi River we saw two British officers, accompanied by a handful *askaris*, walking slowly down the road. They were holding up a pole with a white piece of cloth flying on top. This was something we had never seen before and we were perplexed. The enemy was walking, slightly hesitantly, straight towards us, holding up a white flag.

General von Lettow ordered us to hold our fire. This was also very peculiar. But we had learned over the past years to obey orders without question and we knew the general to be a wise and intelligent man. We kept these two British officers in our sights but held our fire. The general sent two German officers out to meet them. They stood and talked for a while in the middle of the road. Then the officers approached the general himself.

The war was over.

They informed General von Lettow that an armistice had been signed in Europe. They further informed him that all fighting was to cease and that he, General von Lettow-Vorbeck, was to lay down his arms and surrender to the Imperial British Army.

Although the general had gleaned an inkling of this news from a recently captured British messenger, he was nevertheless visibly stunned.

For four long years he had fought battles that were lost before they began and still he had not surrendered—years in which he and his men had traversed land so hostile and had endured hardships so unimaginable that only by the grace of God did we stand here now in front of these British officers—years in which we had resisted, not only superior British forces, but all manner of pestilence ... wild animals, crocodile-infested waters, drought, famine, malaria, tsetse fly ... and now, weapons laid down, no imminent assault, no battle on the rise ...

... and on this dusty road basked in sunshine, he was being asked to surrender.

He would not believe it.

The British officers shook their heads and informed the general that they would go back to Chambesi to return shortly with the telegram containing the news of armistice dispatched by a certain Mr. Croad. A few hours later they were back, with the official telegram. They presented it to the general and only then did he accept that Germany had been defeated.

We were summoned from our positions in the bush and formally informed of the devastating news.

For the first time in my life the harsh African sun chilled my flesh and I shuddered in its heat. My throat was tight and my saliva had dried up. I tried to swallow but the muscles in the back of my throat constricted. The hand of defeat, of shame, gripped me so tightly that I thought I would vomit and collapse, but I did not. I stood straight and tall, my head held high. The shocking news had drained my face, drained my spirit but Allah was at my side that day. I could only imagine how the general must have been feeling, though he too stood straight and tall, his God at his side.

General von Lettow then advised us that we were to accompany the British officers to Chambesi in order to officially lay down our arms. His words drifted dreamily over me and clung to the air around me. I was vaguely aware of falling in and marching to Chambesi. The cloud of disbelief and uncertainty cleared a fraction when we were met on the northern banks of the Chambesi by a number of senior British officers. Here they read out the terms of surrender to General von Lettow.

The general had no option but to accept.

He was standing at the head of our column, his officers behind him. The sun hung low in the western sky, suspended as if it too had paused in its descent to witness this moment. Nothing moved, no bird chirped, no breeze rustled through the scrub. Africa held her breath while this great soldier surrendered his sword—this man who had for four years held off overwhelming British forces—sometimes swollen to one hundred and thirty thousand in number—with at most fourteen thousand soldiers, thirteen thousand of whom were *askaris*, though at the time of our surrender our numbers had dwindled to less than five thousand

As he drew his sword from its scabbard, its immaculate surface caught the last light of the day and a sliver of sharp light was thrown across his face and across the tear that lay unspilled in his eye. Holding the sword by its blade he handed it to the senior British officer.

The general was ordered to instruct his men to lay down their arms, in a pile on the side of the road. He turned around. His face held nothing but pride as he looked upon us and relayed the instruction. He seemed to sense our turmoil and although his voice was strong and unwavering, his eyes held a kindly glow. One by one we stepped forward, unshouldered our rifles, loosened our ammunition belts and dropped them by the side of the dusty road.

The war was well and truly over.

We spent two days at Chambesi after which the general and his German officers were taken north to Abercorn. The *askari* troops were marched under separate escort, as prisoners of war, to Abercorn. When all were gathered, General von Lettow was called to a certain spot at the edge of town where he formally signed the documents of surrender.

This was the last time I was to see him, the man who had fought at our side since 1915. He was taken away and we were given to understand that he had been sent back to Europe.

The German *askaris* were disbanded and we were given orders to return to our homelands.

Most of us returned to Tanganyika through the Ufipa country across the valley of the Rukwa. During the journey home memories of my childhood came flooding back, of happy days of exploration and adventure. This journey, with its memories and beauty, restored my weakened spirit and I found my foot-fall lightening.

And I returned, once again, to Tabora.

Much of Tabora had been destroyed during the war. Many old houses and landmarks were gone. The *boma* we had built so long ago still stood—the German flag now replaced by the British flag that fluttered above. On the hills west of Tabora were a large number of war graves —Belgian, German and British soldiers. Early in the war the Belgians had advanced on Tabora after a great battle that had taken place twelve miles west of the town. Tabora had fallen.

The advent of the British in our country caused much confusion. They took over the administration and introduced British rule, once again with strange new laws and customs.

The British were not the savage masters the Germans were and a completely new era was ushered in.

EPILOGUE

With my return home and under this new regime I found that life continued much as it had done before, yet we were no longer molested by those who presumed themselves in power. Before the time of the Germans I had been a nobleman from a wealthy family of much standing. My mother and father had since passed on, into the realm of Mohammed. Now I found myself a humble man, of no standing at all. However, even as a poor man, life for me was easier and more pleasant under British rule.

The British were slack authoritarians. They removed the hereditary tribal authority from the chiefs, causing many people to turn against and flout the law. All power was taken from the people of the villages and vested in the hands of the British administrators. Thieves would steal and yet be freed for lack of evidence, their cases dismissed by the district commissioner.

As a result rogues and vagabonds appeared in our midst. Gone were the days when wrongdoers were severely punished by the chiefs or the Arabs or the Germans. Under the new, softer governance of Britain, punishment consisted of being sent to gaol for a time. There you would be fed, clothed, looked after, perhaps made to work in the fields, and then released. No lessons were learned through this method of punishment.

Moral standards were corroded and the laws of Mohammed that had been so strictly obeyed in the past, our code for living as a people, were continually spurned and disregarded.

Years passed, during which time I worked on various sisal estates in different parts of the country. I joined the British colonial police but found I had tired of such service. I left to work on a farm where I stayed for many years.

Eventually I returned to my village, which had moved from Tabora to the Usenge district, and there I made a living, as did many others, collecting wild honey and melting down the combs for beeswax for which there was great demand. I hunted too, and although illegal, I shot many elephants and sold the ivory to the Arab and Indian traders who paid well and asked no questions.

I lived in peace and comfort, paying my taxes annually, when one day I heard that the Locust Control Department was looking for scouts—people who knew the country and where were situated the breeding grounds of the dreaded red locust.

I applied and was selected as a scout for the Usenge area.

With his foot Old Ali nudged a log into the fire, causing sparks and smoke to rise into the night sky. Suddenly the dwindling fire burst into flame, throwing shadows of the past against the backdrop of Africa. In the embers slaves, manacled together, trudged towards a thundering train that was thrashing its way through the African bush … and then, flickering in the coals, the canvas drifted into one of marching soldiers. The images dissolved and left an old man, silent now, rousing himself from the past into the present where he sat, among friends.

For Mzee Ali tomorrow was another day and with the passage of time perhaps he would re-tell his story in the company of Allah's heaven.

POSTSCRIPT

General Paul von Lettow-Vorbeck returned to Germany in January 1919, having spent the two months following armistice in ensuring the *askaris* of his *Schutztruppe* were accorded fair and equal treatment. For the next twenty years he was involved in right-wing politics, though always staunchly anti-Nazi.

After World War II, his old foe, and friend, Jan Smuts, found him living in destitution and, together with a group of fellow British and South African officers, arranged for the general to be paid a modest pension.

In 1959, aged 89, the general returned to Tanganyika where he received a hero's welcome from his surviving *askaris*. It is possible, though unlikely, that Mzee Ali was still alive. On seeing the plight of his *askaris*, the general began lobbying the West German government to acknowledge their role in World War I and to pay them some sort of pension.

On his death in 1964, the German government paid a stipend to the surviving *askaris*. Again, it is unlikely that Mzee Ali was still alive. At the time of publication of this book, it is not known what became of the Mzee after his retirement from the Department of Locust Control. Efforts are ongoing to establish the time and place of his death, and to contact his family.

Monument erected in commemoration of the surrender of General von Lettow-Vorbeck to the British forces.

Bror Ürme MacDonell was born in 1921 in Elizabethville, the Belgian Congo. He was educated in France and later at Eton in England. He became fluent in over a dozen languages including French, Swahili, chiShona and several other African languages. Aged nineteen, he was drafted into service during the Second World War as Regimental Sergeant-Major with the African Light Infantry in East Africa and India and later transferred to Army Intelligence with the Northern Rhodesia Regiment. After the war he took up a varied career in hunting, locust control, farming, African administration and local government, working in the remotest bush of Northern Rhodesia and Tanganyika. He moved to Southern Rhodesia (now Zimbabwe) during the sixties and began writing *Mzee Ali* in 1963, from his campfire 'bush notes' of the forties. (Several UK publishers rejected the manuscript as being "too politically incorrect"—presumably because of the references to the black-on-black slave-trading.) He retired to the South Coast of KwaZulu-Natal, where he died in 1998. He is survived by his wife Marjorie and four children.

Kerrin Cocks is a journalist by profession and has worked in the military-history publishing industry for twelve years. She ghostwrote *Mzee Ali: The Biography of an African Slave-raider Turned Askari and Scout* (30° South, 2006) and conceptualized the *Africa@War* series (co-published by 30° South and Helion & Co.). In 2009 she scripted, directed, produced and edited the full-length DVD documentary that accompanied Richard Wood's book *Counter-Strike from the Sky: The Rhodesian All-arms Fireforce in the War in the Bush, 1974–1980*, which was bought and aired on the New Zealand Documentary Channel. In 2010 she produced a short documentary on the SADF Pathfinder Company, founded by Colonel Jan Breytenbach and ably led by Sergeant-Major Pete McAleese. She has edited, proofread and/or commissioned in excess of a hundred military history titles. She is an honorary member of the Rhodesian Light Infantry Regimental Association.